Between
COMPROMISE
— and —
COURAGE

The Choice Every Christian Must Make

SECOND EDITION

© 2024 Denison Ministries

Scripture quotations are from the ESV® Bible (The Holy Bible, English Standard Version®), copyright © 2001 by Crossway, a publishing ministry of Good News Publishers. Used by permission. All rights reserved.

Scripture quotations marked (NIV) are taken from the Holy Bible, New International Version®, NIV®. Copyright © 1973, 1978, 1984, 2011 by Biblica, Inc.™ Used by permission of Zondervan. All rights reserved worldwide. www.zondervan.com The "NIV" and "New International Version" are trademarks registered in the United States Patent and Trademark Office by Biblica, Inc.™

ALSO FROM DENISON FORUM

The Daily Article email newsletter is news discerned differently every Monday through Friday.
Subscribe for free at DenisonForum.org.

Matthew: A Guide to Genuine Discipleship

Awaken My Heart: A Lent Devotional

Bold Faith

The Path To Purpose

The Fifth Great Awakening and the Future of America

How Does God See America?

What Are My Spiritual Gifts?

A Light Unto My Path: A Practical Guide to Studying the Bible

How to Bless God by Blessing Others: Words of Wisdom from the Early Church to Christians Today

**Request these books and more at
DenisonForum.org/store**

TABLE OF CONTENTS

CHAPTER 1   5
JESUS IS COMING SOON, RIGHT?
What does the Bible say about the end times?

CHAPTER 2   25
THE CONTROVERSY OF BEING LEFT BEHIND:
What does the Bible say about the rapture?

CHAPTER 3   45
DEFENDING YOURSELF WITHOUT ATTACKING YOUR WITNESS: What does the Bible say about self-defense and gun control?

CHAPTER 4   65
"THE GLEAMING FUTURISTIC LAND OF OZ":
What does the Bible say about artificial intelligence?

CHAPTER 5   79
THE PARDONABLE SIN:
What does the Bible say about suicide?

CHAPTER 6   109
THE MORAL ISSUE OF OUR TIME:
What does the Bible say about abortion?

CHAPTER 7   145
THE GREATEST SIN IN AMERICA:
What does the Bible say about racism?

CHAPTER 8   171
THE CALL TO TRANSFORMATIONAL GOOD:
What does the Bible say about politics and religious liberty?

Introduction

Today, our culture teaches that the benchmark of civility and the highest moral good to which we can strive is *tolerance*. Of course, tolerance means different things to different people. In reality, our shared cultural definition of tolerance often plays out in this way: you are welcome to your beliefs unless someone disagrees. If anyone considers your beliefs to be hurtful to anyone, they must therefore be hurtful. And if they are hurtful, they must be disallowed.

And that is rarely the case to a greater extent than when those beliefs pertain to God.

However, this choice between compromise and courage is not new for God's people.

Think of the prophet Jeremiah, imprisoned in a cistern because he would not stop preaching God's word (Jeremiah 38:1–6). Remember Shadrach, Meshach, and Abednego in the fiery furnace (Daniel 3), Daniel in the lions' den (Daniel 6), Peter in Herod's prison (Acts 12), and John exiled on Patmos (Revelation 1).

The compromise we will be encouraged to make was just what the apostles were ordered to do by the Supreme Court of their day: "We strictly charged you not to teach in this name, yet here you have filled Jerusalem with your teaching" (Acts 5:28). If these believers would keep their beliefs to themselves and go along to get along, they would get along. However, the apostles replied: "<u>We must obey God rather than men</u>" (v. 29). When the council then "beat them and charged them not to speak in the name of Jesus" (v. 40), they left "rejoicing that they were counted worthy to suffer dishonor for the name" (v. 41).

Standing for biblical truth does not mean that we condemn others or consider ourselves to be better than them. It means that we love them enough to tell them the truth even—and especially—when they do not want to hear it. It means that we share with them the good news that has given us hope in the belief that it will do the same for them.

It's my hope and prayer that this book provides you with the truth of what the Bible says on eight topics that continue to divide the church from the culture and, at times, Christians from one another:

- eschatology
- the rapture
- self-defense and gun control
- artificial intelligence
- suicide
- abortion
- racism
- and religious liberty

Note that the Bible speaks more clearly on some of these subjects than on others. However, in each case, learning how to have the conversation in a way that fosters a biblically grounded sense of community while—most importantly—keeping our focus on God's truth above all else is crucial to presenting our faith well in today's culture. You may note that issues pertaining to sexuality are not listed; because that topic is so expansive, we are writing a standalone book on what the Bible says about sexuality.

Please know that some of these chapters are adapted and updated from content previously published at DenisonForum.org. However, each chapter within this book also includes discussion questions for personal or small group study intended to help you process and apply the truth of Scripture on these important topics.

Additionally, you're reading a revised and expanded version of the first edition of *Between Compromise and Courage*. We removed chapters on removing statues and cancel culture; they can be found on our website at DenisonForum.org by searching for those terms. We did so in order to speak to other topics that we have routinely received questions about, e.g., the end times, gun control, and artificial intelligence.

When you next face the choice between compromise and courage, may these words and God's Spirit encourage you to boldness.

—Dr. Jim Denison

1

JESUS IS COMING SOON, RIGHT?

What does the Bible say about the end times?

Questions about the "end times" are among the most common in Christian doctrine. Theologians call the issue *eschatology*, meaning "a word about last things." The area deals with such questions as the Second Coming and the nature of hell and heaven. In this chapter, we're going to focus mostly on the way Christians have approached those questions across our history before taking a closer look at one of the more contentious elements of that conversation—the rapture—in the next chapter. So with that approach in mind, let's start a quick overview of how people have attempted to answer these questions across Christian history.

Many of the first Christians thought Jesus' return would happen in their lifetime. Even as that belief began to fade, they still anticipated his coming with each new generation. As we'll discuss later, that expectation changed when Constantine legalized the faith and Christians began to think they could bring the kingdom of heaven to earth before Christ's return. However, there were always those who thought their actions would either bring about the second coming or that the world was devolving to the point that Jesus must surely return before all was lost.

During the sixteenth century, for example, Martin Luther thought the Pope was the Antichrist and expected Jesus' return during his lifetime. Conversely, Christopher Columbus thought the world would end in 1656 and that his explorations would lead a Christian army in the final crusade to convert the world.

William Miller, the founder of the Adventists, preached that Jesus would return in 1843. When that didn't happen, he left the movement, but his followers later decided he'd been partially correct and God had begun the process of evaluating and judging the world but simply had not yet returned.

Charles Taze Russell, the founder of the Jehovah's Witnesses, came out of Miller's Adventist tradition and sold all of his business interests in anticipation of Christ's return in 1878. When that didn't happen, he began preaching that Christ had returned spiritually but that the end of the world wouldn't happen until 1914. When World War I started that year, his prediction looked good. But, as the calendar rolled to 1915 and beyond, his mistake was made clear to all. He died shortly thereafter.

However, the failures of Miller and Russell to accurately predict the end of the world did not dissuade others from trying.

Harold Camping wrote the bestselling book *1994?* in which he predicted the end would come on September 6, 1994. He again made news by predicting the end would come on May 21, 2011. Edgar Whisenant published *88*

Reasons Why the Rapture Will Be in 1988 and sold thousands of copies. Trinity Broadcasting Network president Paul Crouch predicted an apocalyptic event for June 9, 1994.

Such predictions will continue because every believer wants to know: When will Jesus come back? Our question is not new, but it will remain relevant until Christ returns and settles the matter.

So with that context in mind, let's turn our attention to a deeper examination of two questions: When will Jesus return? And how should we view the end times?

WHEN WILL JESUS RETURN?

After his resurrection, Jesus appeared to his disciples over a period of forty days and taught them about the kingdom of God (Acts 1:3). He then promised them the Holy Spirit (v. 5). They knew that the coming of the Spirit and the coming of the kingdom were related. So in response, they asked the question Christians have been asking ever since: "Lord, will you at this time restore the kingdom to Israel?" (v. 6).

Their question was logical but wrong. About this verse John Calvin said, "There are as many errors in this question as words" (*Institutes* 1.29).

Jesus said, "It is not for you to know times or seasons that the Father has fixed by his own authority" (v. 7). "Times or seasons" refers to specific dates as well as years. "Not for you" refers to Jesus' first and closest disciples: Peter, James, John, the others, and even Mary and Jesus' brothers.

If Jesus wouldn't tell them when he would return, would he tell you and me?

If discovering the time of his return was possible by scriptural exegesis or spiritual commitment, would they not have determined it? To say that we know what Peter, James, John, and Mary didn't know is egotism, to say the least.

The Father has placed this decision in his authority alone. Jesus said, "But concerning that day or that hour, no one knows, not even the angels in heaven, nor the Son, but only the Father. Be on guard, keep awake. For you do not know when the time will come" (Mark 13:32–33). Paul told us that Jesus' coming would be as surprising and unanticipated as a "thief in the night" (1 Thessalonians 5:2). Peter made the same prediction (2 Peter 3:10).

Listen to Jesus' warning:

> Stay dressed for action and keep your lamps burning, and be like men who are waiting for their master to come home from the wedding feast, so that they may open the door to him at once when he comes and knocks. . . . If he comes in the second watch, or in the third, and finds them awake, blessed are those servants! But know this, that if the master of the house had known at what hour the thief was coming, he would not have left his house to be broken into. You also must be ready, for the Son of Man is coming at an hour you do not expect (Luke 12:35–36, 38–40).

No one but God knows when Jesus will return.

We must be ready every day, for it could be any day. This is the clear teaching of God's word and must be the foundation of any efforts to understand the end times.

Yet Christ did speak of signs that would precede his coming, and Christians have been weighing events in their time against those signs ever since.

THE FOUR SIGNS THAT SIGNAL JESUS' RETURN

In one of his final lessons to his disciples prior to the crucifixion, Jesus told them of four signs that would precede the end times:

1. Jesus warns that "many will come in my name, saying, 'I am the Christ,' and they will lead many astray" (Matthew 24:5).

2. Jesus promised that we "will hear of wars and rumors of wars . . . For nation will rise against nation, and kingdom against kingdom" (v. 6–7)

3. Jesus said "there will be famines and earthquakes in various places" (v. 7). Moreover, the account in Luke's gospel speaks of "pestilences . . . . terrors and great signs from heaven" as well (Luke 21:11).

4. Finally, Christ warned that "they will deliver you [Christians] up to tribulation and put you to death, and you will be hated by all nations for my name's sake" (Matthew 24:9).

But if we can't know when Jesus will return, what good are the signs? After all, evidence of these precursors to the end times has existed in most every generation for the last two thousand years, and Jesus still hasn't come back.

The reason we were given these signs, as with most prophecies, is to give us hope and encouragement in the midst of such troubles.

When we look at wars, persecution, and other calamities with any sense of assurance that this sign is *the* sign, we're making a mistake. Yet, knowing that our Lord promised such events would take place and that, ultimately, they will either pass or result in his return should give us the perspective necessary to persevere in the midst of them.

God's goal is that when the world seems like it's falling apart, his people won't. Instead, we should continue to share the gospel and proclaim Jesus is Lord as we prepare for the day when Christ will return and remove all doubt as to the truth of that statement. With that perspective in mind, let's now ask our second question.

HOW SHOULD WE VIEW THE END TIMES?

Someone once asked a wise older pastor for his view of the end times. He smiled and said, "The Lord put me on the preparation committee, not the planning committee."

The pastor spoke for us all. We cannot control how the Lord chooses to end history. Our theories about the future are just that. The word of God is too practical to focus extensively on an issue that possesses no pragmatic value for our lives. If I could prove a particular theory of the end times to you, would such knowledge change your life today?

Nonetheless, sincere Christians passionately debate these issues. In this section we'll briefly survey the options held by biblical interpreters before focusing on the views most often found among believers today.

However, before we start, it's important to note that these views are more endpoints on a spectrum than distinct camps with clear boundaries. Christians can—and often do—adopt elements of more than one in their understanding of the end times, and that's all right. After all, if Scripture were indisputably clear as to the right approach, we wouldn't still be debating the issue nearly two thousand years later.

Four approaches to reading Revelation

Regarding the book of Revelation, eight approaches find support among evangelical scholars. The first four pertain primarily to how we are to read the letter as a whole, and Revelation is first and foremost a letter written by John to a particular group of Christians. The latter four deal more with how we should interpret the role of the millennium and Christ's return within the larger context of end-times theology.

Preterist

The preterist position asserts that Revelation and other eschatological literature were written primarily for the encouragement of their immediate audiences, not to predict or speak to the future.

Scholars in this tradition emphasize the "apocalyptic" nature of eschatological literature. "Apocalyptic" (from the Greek word for "unveiling") was a popular literary approach from around 200 BC to 200 AD. It used symbolic, visionary, and dramatic elements to convey encouragement and hope to persecuted people.

Preterists argue that Revelation matches every description of "apocalyptic" literature except that it names its author ("apocalyptic" writings are typically pseudonymous). And so they interpret Revelation as we understand Philippians: as a first-century book with perennial spiritual application. They would not see the book or other eschatological literature as predictive in nature but as intended first for their original, persecuted audiences.

If tradition is correct and John did write Revelation while imprisoned on Patmos, it would make sense that he would want to couch both his condemnation of Rome and his encouragement for Christians to remain faithful in the face of persecution in language that his guards could not clearly discern. As such, a primary benefit of the preterist approach is how it helps us pay attention to the letter's larger context and teachings rather than viewing every facet of the book through the lens of eschatology. A great deal of practical and time-honored truth is contained within Revelation that we would miss if the only parts we studied were those that seemed to describe an event that has yet to occur.

The preterist approach falls short, however, if it is treated as the only lens through which the letter should be read. While many—perhaps even most—of the teachings in Revelation are meant to encourage and guide Christians living in any age, there are also clear implications for the end times that should not be overlooked. So let's continue by examining another approach that can offer some guidance as well.

Spiritual principles

A second interpretive method views eschatological texts with regard to spiritual principles. It sees Revelation and other literature as teaching spiritual facts (e.g., good will triumph, God's people must persevere, etc.) but does not relate these passages to specific historical events or issues.

The benefit of this approach is that it emphasizes the more timeless truths contained within the letter and demonstrates its relevance to believers in all generations rather than just those who happen to be alive during the end times. And to be sure, many aspects of Revelation are best read symbolically.

However, this view shares the limitations of the preterist approach while also opening believers to the dangers of over-allegorizing the letter's message. Historically, Christians have often crossed the line into heresy when attempting to nail down the true meaning of the more symbolic elements of Scripture. Advocates of this approach must be careful not to make the same mistake. A good principle to keep in mind when reading any book of the Bible is that the text can never mean what it never meant. Any interpretation that would have been irrelevant or incomprehensible to the book's original audience is likely flawed.

Historicist

A third approach is known as the historicist perspective. It sees Revelation and other eschatological texts as forecasting the development of history but also argues that history tends to repeat itself. As such, while specific events through history may appear to align well with what John describes, that hardly makes them unique as you typically do not have to search very hard to find examples of similar events from the past.

The benefit of this approach is that history is cyclical in the sense that human nature does not change. Many of the wars, conflicts, and sins that reside at the heart of Revelation's message do appear again and again through the ages. Understanding that not every war is necessarily *the* war simply because it bears some resemblance to what John wrote can grant an important sense of perspective as we try to move through the course of our lives. Moreover, it can serve as a powerful reminder of why every generation needs Jesus, regardless of whether they are walking closer to the Lord or further away from him.

A danger inherent to this approach (and the next approach we'll discuss) is the temptation to think that the present generation is the one on the cusp of history's conclusion. Believers who take the historicist perspective have, at times, fallen into that trap and began not only to look for evidence of Christ's return but also to actively live as though they were certain it was imminent. In so doing, they have often lost sight of the very perspective that the approach was meant to give.

In addition, the historicist approach can also breed the opposite problem, lulling people into a false confidence that present events cannot be signs of the end times because similar circumstances have happened in the past without ending in the Lord's return. While no one who believed the end times were upon them has been correct to date, eventually it will happen, and Scripture is abundantly clear that we are to live perpetually with the knowledge that it could be today.

Futurist

The final perspective on how we are to read the letter as a whole is the futurist approach. Where adherents of the preterist perspective view Revelation through the lens of the first century, interpreting John's visions as apocalyptic symbolism, the futurist position sees them as a literal account of what will occur in those final days.

Proponents of this view argue that we should take John at his word when he writes that he was given a vision of heaven and told to record everything that he saw

(Revelation 1:11, 4:1). As such, while he may have had trouble portraying his experiences in a way that is easily understood by those who have not yet shared them, the events of Revelation should be seen as the literal truth of what awaits those alive during the tribulation rather than as symbolic or poetic attempts to convey spiritual truths.

The benefit of this approach is that it helps readers take seriously the promise at the letter's end, that "blessed is the one who keeps the words of the prophecy of this book" by avoiding the temptation to over-spiritualize or allegorize the text beyond its intended meaning (Revelation 22:7). While the other approaches are certainly capable of taking the text seriously as well, Revelation's most ardent readers are often those who take a futurist perspective to the writing.

The danger of adopting this perspective to the book, however, is that it can lead readers to be constantly searching headlines and news for ways that current events fit in John's vision.

Because even proponents of the futurist approach admit that John's records can be difficult to decipher and, ultimately, represent an attempt to do the impossible by describing the indescribable, some translation has to take place in order to understand how those visions will play out. Consequently, those who favor this view must guard against the temptation to look so hard for signs of Christ's return or the dawn of the tribulation that they miss the ways in which God is currently at work in the world around them. Moreover, even an attempt at reading the text literally does not insulate a person from the same kinds of mistakes in interpretation and the need for humility that are inherent to each of these approaches.

And that humility is particularly important when it comes to how we should understand one of the more divisive elements of eschatological beliefs: the millennium.

FOUR APPROACHES TO THE MILLENNIUM

The next four approaches focus in various ways on the "millennium," the thousand-year reign of Christ on earth described in Revelation 20:1–6. When many Christians think of eschatology, this subject and the rapture, which will be discussed in the next chapter, are the topics that come to mind first. They are also among the most controversial and potentially divisive elements of the conversation.

As such, we want to remind you once again that having the correct end-times theology is not an essential doctrine of the Christian faith, and chances are good that all of us will be wrong in our understanding of at least some facets of how these events play out. So embark upon this conversation with a heavy dose of humility and prayerfully ask the Lord to help you understand which aspects of these approaches are most closely aligned with the truth of Scripture.

Amillennialism

This approach (from the Greek word *a* for "no") argues that there will be no literal millennium. Many sympathetic to this view find seven cycles within the book of Revelation, each descriptive of life on earth from Jesus' ascension to his return. For them, Israel is the church today awaiting the second coming of our Lord, but the parts of Revelation that speak of the millennium should be read figuratively rather than literally.

Historically, starting from the time of Augustine through much of the Middle Ages and Reformation, an amillennial approach—or some mixture of amillennialism with postmillennial undertones—was the predominant view of the church. Their argument is that Christ has already inaugurated his kingdom but his dominion will not be complete until he returns again to establish his reign for all eternity.

The benefit of this approach is that it offers some protection against becoming so focused on what is to come that we miss opportunities to help expand God's kingdom in the present. While there is merit to C. S. Lewis' statement that "if you read history you will find that the Christians who did most for the present world were just those who thought most of the next," the old saying that "some people are so heavenly minded that they are no earthly good" is also often correct.

The truth is that Scripture—and particularly the book of Revelation—call us to live in the awareness of what's to come without becoming so fixated on it that we lose sight of all that God has called us to do until that future arrives. The amillennial perspective can help with the latter but carries with it many of the problems inherent to a more symbolic reading of Scripture.

Postmillennialism

Postmillennialism, at its core, is the belief that Jesus will return following a literal millennium. In this belief, it bears much in common with amillennialism. In fact, up until the early 1900s the two views were not recognized as being distinct. Prior to that, amillennialists tended to view themselves as postmillennialists.

The primary distinction between the two views is that postmillennialism teaches that, prior to the second coming, the church will transform the culture and make it more like the kingdom of heaven that Scripture describes. Persecution will abate while humanity becomes more aligned with God's will and a biblical worldview.

Elements of this belief can be seen as far back as the fourth century, when Constantine's rise to power, legalization of the Christian faith, and then efforts to promote the faith throughout a predominately pagan culture led many believers to think that the church was on its way to transforming that culture into the kingdom of heaven. Historical writings by figures like Eusebius of Caesarea—in which Constantine was portrayed just short of the second coming in his own right—contributed greatly to that perspective as well. The church then continued to push the idea that their efforts to conform the world into Christ's likeness were essential to the Lord's return across the ensuing centuries.

As the church began to resemble that kingdom less and less throughout the Middle Ages, some question as to its eschatological role crept in. However, ultimately most believed that the church still had a direct role to play in preparing the world for Christ's return. It was just that their understanding of what constituted the church began to morph from the Catholic Church to the larger body of Christ. So believers worked to reform the faith, improve society, and train others to do the same. Some of the most impactful seminaries in America, for example, were founded by people who thought doing so would hasten the second coming.

It really was not until the Civil War began to fracture the way in which many Americans saw our society that many Christians began to give up on the notion that the culture could ever sufficiently represent Christ's kingdom before Christ's return. And that trend was only exacerbated when two world wars followed in the next century.

Today, postmillennialism remains one of the dominant eschatological approaches within Christianity, though its popularity has certainly waned from its previous heights.

Premillennialism

Premillennialism argues that Jesus will return to earth prior to the millennium, though debate remains about what that return will look like. The various branches of premillennialism agree that Jesus will come back after a period of tribulation, but whether believers will have to endure that tribulation (the historical premillennialist position) or will be raptured out of it at some point (the dispensationalist perspective) remains a subject of debate.

However, regardless of the timing and nature of the rapture (the subject of the next chapter), premillennialists agree that once that reign begins, it will last for a thousand years after which point Satan will escape his bondage and be vanquished, inaugurating the eternal reign of Christ.

Historically, something approaching this view was the presumption in many circles for the first three centuries of the church. The first generations of Christians believed that Jesus would return in their lifetime, which is thought to be one of the reasons why Paul had to remind the Thessalonian Christians of their need to work (2 Thessalonians 3:6–12).

Once enough time passed that the early believers began to revise that expectation, the general understanding remained that Jesus would have to return before their world could begin to resemble the kingdom of heaven. Justin Martyr and Irenaeus—two of the most significant theologians and apologists of the early church—both argued for some form of premillennial reign prior to the final resurrection and dawn of eternity. Given that, at this point in its history, Christianity was an illegal and persecuted—albeit growing—faith, their doubts as to the culture ever changing to the degree described in Scripture are understandable.

While the dramatic changes that accompanied Constantine's legalization and promotion of the faith changed the perspective throughout the ensuing centuries, momentum toward a premillennial approach began to build again during the seventeenth and eighteenth centuries as many revivalist leaders began to move away from the amillennial and postmillennial perspectives. However, it was not until the end of the 1700s and the start of the Second Great Awakening that premillennialism really began to gain traction in the church, and even then it was primarily among evangelicals.

It was also during this era that the dispensationalist version of premillennialism began to grow in popularity. The primary differences between a more historical premillennialism and its dispensationalist counterpart will be examined in greater depth next. However, these variations within a premillennial belief reiterate the fact that a great deal of diversity exists even within most of these approaches. To speak of the various eschatological camps as if there are always clear, never-intersecting boundaries between them would be false. With that truth in mind, we'll turn our attention to the final approach.

Dispensational premillennialism

Dispensational premillennialism—more commonly referred to as just dispensationalism—views Revelation and other eschatological texts primarily as a forecast of the very last days of history. As such, there are a number of teachings that may not seem inherently eschatological but still play an important role in their understanding of the end times.

One such teaching is that Israel and the church are distinct, meaning that the new covenant of Christianity did not replace God's old covenant with Israel. Moreover, the church is not the continuation of that promised relationship. Consequently, dispensationalists teach that any promises made to Israel in the Old Testament have been or will be fulfilled literally with Israel.

Interpreters using this approach divide history into "dispensations," i.e., various time periods during which God dealt with humanity in different ways. Jesus will "rapture" the church out of the world—though there is some disagreement as to when that rapture will occur—so that God can return to his work with Israel during the "Great Tribulation." This period will culminate in Jesus' return to earth and the millennium (thus "premillennialism"), followed by the final judgment and eternity in heaven or hell.

Dispensationalism came to America through the writings and sermons of British pastor John Nelson Darby during the late 1800s, but it rose to prominence through the preaching of St. Louis pastor James Brookes and, to an extent, famed evangelist D. L. Moody. Then, in 1909, Cyrus Scofield published one of the first study Bibles and included notes throughout explaining how the various parts of Scripture fit within a dispensationalist model.

A host of Bible colleges, institutes, and seminaries then trained generations of pastors to see Scripture through that lens as well. And while other forms of evangelicalism grew to prominence across the same period of time, some of the most influential leaders within the evangelical church have approached Scripture from the dispensationalist perspective.

That said, it remains only one of many approaches people can take to understanding the end times. Like the other approaches described in this chapter, both its supporters and those who think differently can find biblically valid reasons for their interpretation.

And that is particularly true for what is often the most controversial element of premillennial theology and the subject of our next chapter: the rapture.

A DISCUSSION GUIDE ON THE END TIMES

1. When you read about all the people in the past who have confidently and incorrectly guessed when Jesus will return, how does it impact the way you think we should approach that question today?

2. In your experience, how have most Christians responded when the news of the day appears to line up with the signs Jesus spoke of in Matthew 24? In light of what is discussed in this chapter, how should Christians respond in those instances?

3. Does the notion that the various theological approaches to the end times are more endpoints on a spectrum than firm camps with clear boundaries change the way you see this conversation? If so, in what ways?

4. Of the four approaches to reading Revelation, which do you find most convincing? Why? Are there elements from the other three approaches that seem correct as well?

5. Of the four approaches to the millennium, which do you find most convincing? Why? Are there elements from the other three approaches that seem correct as well?

6. In light of what is discussed in this chapter, how should Christians engage with eschatology both theologically and in conversation with other believers? What are some productive ways we can participate in that discussion while drawing ourselves and others closer to the Lord?

2

THE CONTROVERSY OF BEING LEFT BEHIND

What does the Bible say about the rapture?

As outlined in the previous chapter, the rapture—as a distinct event from the second coming—is primarily a doctrine held by dispensationalists. In its simplest form, the rapture is the belief that before Jesus comes back as the returning king and establishes his dominion, he will first come back to take his followers out of the world. In dispensationalist theology, the purpose is twofold.

First, removing the church clears the path for Jesus to begin fulfilling the old covenant with Israel. Remember, dispensationalists believe that the church is not the continuation of God's people but rather a second branch in biblical history built on the new covenant in Christ. They teach that the Lord still has to fulfill his previous promises to a literal Israel, though, and that can't happen if the church is still around.

The rapture, then, clears the way for God to judge the world and bring Israel to salvation.

Second, removing the church spares Christians from having to endure either all or part of the tribulation, the series of divine judgments described in Revelation 6–16.

Some debate exists among dispensationalists as to when the church will be removed, with the traditional view setting the rapture at the beginning, but an increasing number are favoring a time later in the tribulation. Wherever one falls on that spectrum, however, this element of Christians essentially disappearing from the earth is likely the first thing most people think of when discussing the rapture. The *Left Behind* series by Tim LaHaye and Jerry B. Jenkins has done much to popularize the view, and it's one reason why a belief in the rapture has become common even among those who do not think of themselves as dispensationalists.

But while the view has become popular, is it biblical?

It turns out that can be a difficult question to answer as well. Yet, by studying a few key passages upon which the belief is built, we can get a better understanding of why it remains among the most pivotal and most controversial aspects of end times theology.

We will start with the passage that deals most directly with the rapture itself before turning our attention to three verses to which people often point as a promise that the church will not endure the tribulation.

AN ESSENTIAL RAPTURE PASSAGE

In 1 Thessalonians 4:13–18, Paul writes:

> But we do not want you to be uninformed, brothers, about those who are asleep, that you may not grieve as others do who have no hope. For since we believe that Jesus died and rose again, even so, through Jesus, God will bring with him those who have fallen asleep.
>
> For this we declare to you by a word from the Lord, that we who are alive, who are left until the coming of the Lord, will not precede those who have fallen asleep. For the Lord himself will descend from heaven with a cry of command, with the voice of an archangel, and with the sound of the trumpet of God. And the dead in Christ will rise first.
>
> Then we who are alive, who are left, will be caught up together with them in the clouds to meet the Lord in the air, and so we will always be with the Lord. Therefore encourage one another with these words.

At the start of chapter 5 he concludes:

> Now concerning the times and the seasons, brothers, you have no need to have anything written to you. For you yourselves are fully aware that the day of the Lord will come like a thief in the night. While people are saying, "There is peace and security," then sudden destruction will come upon them as labor pains come upon a pregnant woman, and they will not escape.

> But you are not in darkness, brothers, for that day to surprise you like a thief. For you are all children of light, children of the day. We are not of the night or of the darkness.
>
> So then let us not sleep, as others do, but let us keep awake and be sober. For those who sleep, sleep at night, and those who get drunk, are drunk at night. But since we belong to the day, let us be sober, having put on the breastplate of faith and love, and for a helmet the hope of salvation.
>
> For God has not destined us for wrath, but to obtain salvation through our Lord Jesus Christ, who died for us so that whether we are awake or asleep we might live with him. Therefore encourage one another and build one another up, just as you are doing.

This section of Scripture is the passage most frequently seen as describing the rapture, a term which comes from the Latin word *rapturo*, which means "caught up" (1 Thessalonians 4:17). But before we dive into the ways in which biblically faithful Christians can and do disagree on the implications of this passage, let's start by looking at three aspects upon which we should all be able to agree.

First, regardless of what eschatological implications one sees in Paul's teaching across these verses, his primary purpose had less to do with end times theology than pastoral care.

He wanted to give a sense of hope and perspective to those grieving over the death of their fellow believers and who were concerned about what those who had already passed will experience when Jesus returns—which, remember, most of them expected to happen in their lifetime.

The apostle's call to grieve with hope and the assurance that those who have passed will share in the glory of that resurrection is meant to help all Christians, from the first century to today, understand that we can trust God with the fate of those who die in Christ. And while it is appropriate to mourn their loss, we do so with the knowledge that the separation is only temporary. As we continue to discuss the implications of this passage and the various ways in which it is interpreted, we must not lose sight of the larger pastoral purpose for which it was originally written.

Second, the assurance we can have in Christ regarding our eternal fate should not lessen the degree to which we strive to live every day in a way that honors him and enhances our witness to others.

It was not an accident that, following his promises of a resurrection and reunion upon Christ's return, Paul immediately spoke about how we should live in light of that eventuality. While there is room to debate whether Christ's return will happen before or after the tribulation, Scripture is clear that Jesus will come back and that we don't have to know when it will happen to be ready when it does. Any debate over the timing of that return must not distract us from Christ's call to live every day ready for it to occur.

Third, note that Paul ends both blocks of verses with the call to "encourage one another" (4:18, 5:11).

As we prepare to look at the ways in which Christians often disagree about the correct interpretation of these verses, it needs to be stated once again that we must not allow any such disagreement to lead to division. These verses and the subject material they describe are meant to spark in us the desire to encourage one another to a greater faith in God and a greater sense of community in his name. Satan would love nothing more than for this subject to cause us to miss opportunities to share the gospel and help others know Jesus.

So, as we prepare to discuss the rapture and the degree to which it is a biblically supported doctrine, remember that we can—and likely will—disagree on elements of what these verses mean. However, any understanding that does not lead us to encourage one another to greater fellowship with our fellow believers and with God ultimately falls short of biblical truth. With that premise in mind, let's now turn our attention to the ways in which this passage can be best understood, starting with the argument for the rapture.

ARGUMENTS SUPPORTING THE BELIEF IN A RAPTURE

As described in the previous section, a fundamental belief within dispensationalism is that Israel and the church are distinct and that God has a separate plan for fulfilling his old covenant promises to Israel in the end times. As such, dispensationalists argue that it is necessary to first remove Christians from the world before those promises can be fulfilled. In the context of that belief, passages like 1 Thessalonians 4:13–5:11 offer a biblically defensible explanation for how that shift could occur.

While those who do not support the idea of a rapture see this passage as another perspective on the second coming rather than a distinct event from Christ's final return, there are some key differences in what Paul describes here and how events are portrayed in the more apocalyptic texts like Revelation 19:11–21.

To start, the Revelation text describes how when Christ returns in judgment, he will do so with "the armies of heaven . . . following him on white horses" (Revelation 19:14). By contrast, 1 Thessalonians mentions only Jesus and does not speak of a heavenly host accompanying him.

Moreover, in John's vision, the only people mentioned are those who will be condemned and slain at Christ's coming. Paul, however, focuses on the believers who will meet Jesus upon his return, with the only mention of judgment taking place in his statement that "God has not destined us for wrath, but to obtain salvation through our Lord Jesus Christ" (1 Thessalonians 5:9).

We will discuss the idea that God has promised to spare us from the pain of the tribulation—the way that dispensationalists typically understand the wrath described in this verse—later in this chapter, but for now it is worth noting that the notion is at least defensible from a biblical perspective.

A second piece that dispensationalists often point to as evidence that the events described in Revelation differ from those found in 1 Thessalonians is that the "church"—*ekklesia* in Greek—is not mentioned during the chapters describing the events that will unfold in the tribulation. After the term is used at the end of Revelation 3, it does not appear again until John's final exhortation in 22:16. They argue that the silence regarding the presence of Christians during the events of the tribulation is evidence that they are not there to endure it.

Lastly, one of the common descriptors of Christ's return is that he will come as a "thief in the night" (1 Thessalonians 5:2; Matthew 24:43; Revelation 16:15). The overt display of power described in Revelation 19 can be difficult to reconcile with the imagery of the thief used by Jesus and others. If, however, Paul speaks to more of a secret return at which time Jesus will rapture his followers and take them to heaven either before the time of wrath begins or before it is completed, then this understanding of the analogy makes more sense.

Ultimately, clear arguments can be made in favor of Christ returning first for his followers and then once again upon the conclusion of the tribulation to judge the world. These arguments are biblically based and biblically defensible, and to portray them as otherwise does not do justice to the doctrine or to those who hold it.

That the view is biblically defensible, however, does not mean it is necessarily the most likely or natural reading of these texts. So let's turn our attention now to arguments against the doctrine of a rapture.

ARGUMENTS AGAINST THE RAPTURE

To begin, while there are clear differences in the accounts of Christ's return given in 1 Thessalonians and the more apocalyptic passages, there are no contradictions. It is plausible that each account describes the same event from a different perspective and with a different focus. In fact, this has been the dominant view for the majority of Christian history.

As discussed previously, Paul was writing to comfort Christians who were worried about fellow believers who had already died and to give them hope for the future. By contrast, John and the prophets wrote to describe the judgment of God and the all-powerful nature of Christ in his return. Both can describe the same event.

Moreover, those who disagree with the idea of a rapture argue that contradictions do begin to emerge when studying these passages with the idea of Jesus returning first for the church and then to judge the world. Both 1 Thessalonians and Revelation make clear that when Jesus returns, he will do so in a way that is both public and impossible to miss, with trumpet calls and a loud cry of command. The Greek word Paul used for "cry of command" occurs only in 1 Thessalonians 4:16 in the New Testament, but it is a military term commonly found in extrabiblical texts and refers to the order a general would give to his subordinates.

Such imagery seems out of place with the notion of a secret return and calls into question the idea that the analogy of the thief is meant to speak to any sense of subtlety. Rather, proponents of Christ's return as a single event typically argue that the thief imagery is meant to convey a sense of suddenness or unexpectedness rather than secrecy.

That notion finds further support in 1 Thessalonians 5, where Paul describes the consequences for those who are too preoccupied with acting like the false prophets of old and declaring "peace and security" rather than heeding the Lord's call to repentance and salvation (v. 3). As biblical scholar Dr. Michael Martin describes, "Their moment of judgment comes as a shock, befalling a people who feel secure. It is like the arrival of a thief, unexpected and surprising. These are the very characteristics of that day that should not apply to the church, for the church knows a day of judgment is approaching (v. 4) and therefore should remain faithful and vigilant (vv. 5–11)."

And while that understanding could also fit with an eschatology involving the rapture, we will soon examine why the nature of that judgment seems to point less to the tribulation than to God's final judgment at the end of history. Before we get there, though, we must consider one final argument for why the events of 1 Thessalonians 4 and 5 point to Christ's second coming rather than the rapture.

In 1 Thessalonians 4:17, Paul describes how believers "will be caught up together with them in the clouds to meet the Lord in the air." The Greek word *apantesin*, typically translated as "to meet," offers a crucial bit of context to understanding what will occur. We find it only two other times in the New Testament: in the parable of the ten virgins who are called to "come out to meet" the bridegroom (Matthew 25:6) and when the believers in Rome "came as far as the Forum of Appius and Three Taverns to meet" Paul and his companions in Acts 28:15. In both instances, those who went out "to meet" the arriving person then returned with that person to the place of their arrival. Moreover, this usage mirrors a common practice during Roman times whenever a foreign dignitary would come to a city. Heralds of his coming would leave the city walls to meet him on his way and then return with him to celebrate his arrival and escort him back into the city.

This is how Paul's first-century audience would have understood his writing about Jesus descending from heaven and believers going to meet him in the air. The idea that they would have returned with Christ to heaven rather than Christ return with them to earth would have been foreign to their minds. Instead, the better and more natural reading of this text is that it describes the second coming of Jesus, the final judgment, and all that those events will entail.

If that will be the case, though, and Christians will not be spared the tribulation in whatever form it will eventually take, what are we to make of the passages that seem to describe "the wrath to come" as an event believers will not experience?

WILL CHRISTIANS SUFFER WRATH IN THE END TIMES?

To answer that question, we will turn our attention to three passages that reside at the center of that debate.

1 Thessalonians 5:9

Paul writes of "the wrath to come" on multiple occasions in 1 Thessalonians. In the last section, we briefly discussed the usage in 5:9 where the apostle promised, "For God has not destined us for wrath, but to obtain salvation through our Lord Jesus Christ," but it is worth revisiting in greater depth.

Part of the difficulty in understanding the correct interpretation of this wrath is that it will almost invariably depend on the way in which one sees the passage as a whole. If Paul is writing about a rapture that removes Christians from the earth prior to either all or part of the tribulation, then it makes sense for this wrath to be interpreted in the context of those events. If, however, Paul is speaking of the second coming, then the most natural reading of this text is that the wrath refers to the final judgment and the consequences for those who have rejected salvation in Christ.

Both readings are biblically defensible, but the latter understanding has been favored for much of Christian history. That historical legacy does not inherently make it correct or settle the larger debate, though, which is why we are fortunate that chapter 5 is not the only time the phrase is used.

1 Thessalonians 1:10

Earlier in that same letter to the Thessalonians, Paul spoke highly of the Christians there because they "turned to God from idols to serve the living and true God, and to wait for his Son from heaven, whom he raised from the dead, Jesus who delivers us from the wrath to come" (1 Thessalonians 1:9–10).

Once again, how you see these larger eschatological issues will have a dramatic impact on how you understand the nature of this wrath. However, one element that makes a tribulation-style wrath less plausible is that Paul would not write anything referencing the end times until much later in the letter. Consequently, if he had the tribulation in mind, this promise would likely depend on him having taught about the end times during his initial visit to Thessalonica if it were to have any meaning to his audience at this point in the epistle.

Ultimately, we cannot know if that was the case, but it is generally best to avoid placing too much emphasis on interpretations that require that much conjecture for support. With that uncertainty in mind, we will conclude by looking at one more passage often seen as promising that Christians will not suffer the wrath to come.

Revelation 3:10

In his letter to the church in Philadelphia, John records Christ's promise that "because you have kept my word about patient endurance, I will keep you from the hour of trial that is coming on the whole world, to try those who dwell on the earth" (Revelation 3:10).

Given the larger context of Revelation and nature of the "hour of trial" verbiage, this verse is seen by many as a guarantee that protection from the trials in those final days will be the reward for those believers who endure well the trials they face as a result of their faith in Christ. This understanding fits well within the larger dispensational perspective and is among the stronger arguments in favor of that approach.

The corresponding argument among those who see the passage in a different light, however, centers less on the proper understanding of the trials to come and more on the nature of the protection that the Lord offers.

The Greek phrase "to keep from"—*tereso ek*—occurs only one other time in the New Testament. In John 17:15, Christ prays, "I do not ask that you take them out of the world, but that you keep them from the evil one." While Jesus does not appear to be referencing the end times, it is noteworthy that he asks the Lord to grant his followers spiritual protection rather than physical safety. That distinction is important in Revelation as well, where the preceding part of the Lord's message to the Philadelphian church recognizes the suffering they had already endured for their faith.

As biblical scholar Dr. G. K. Beale notes, "To say that a promise of deliverance from the incomparable physical horrors of a 'great tribulation' is a basis for an exception to the overall [New Testament] view of suffering bears the burden of proof." Scripture is replete with examples of God being willing to allow his people to suffer for their faith and with how that suffering is often redeemed by drawing others to the Lord. It would seem strange for him to change that strategy and remove his witnesses from the world during humanity's last chance to come to salvation.

Moreover, there is biblical evidence that Christians will endure at least part of the tribulation.

The "great multitude that no one could number, from every nation, from all tribes and peoples and languages, standing before the throne and before the Lamb, clothed in white robes, with palm branches in their hands" from Revelation 7:9 were clothed in white because they "are the ones coming out of the great tribulation" and "have washed their robes and made them white in the blood of the Lamb" (Revelation 7:14).

While it is possible the "hour of trial" referenced in Revelation 3 will occur later in the tribulation, it is difficult to see how Christians will escape all of it or why the Lord would prioritize keeping them from physical danger when it would mean placing the lost at even greater spiritual risk.

Ultimately, it is possible that Revelation 3:10 does speak to a promise from God to remove his people from the tribulation, but it is by no means the only plausible interpretation. As such, it seems a fitting way to conclude our examination of the rapture and why it remains one of the more divisive doctrines in the faith.

As we've seen, there are biblically defensible arguments both for and against the rapture. Again, much depends on the theological framework with which we approach these verses, but there is room for Christians to disagree and still remain faithful to Scripture.

We should always strive to have the correct understanding of God's word. However, on issues like these where we cannot be certain what that correct understanding is, it would be a far greater mistake to allow this subject to limit the degree to which we can work in community with those who think differently than to hold the wrong view.

And, considering that none of us will know the full truth of what will happen until Christ returns—either to take us back to heaven or to inaugurate his kingdom on earth—it is not an issue that warrants as much energy and reflection as the more practical elements of how God has called us to live.

So, with that perspective in mind, let's finish by discussing the most beneficial way to frame this conversation within our larger approach to faith.

WHY DOES YOUR VIEW OF THE RAPTURE MATTER RIGHT NOW?

In light of what we've discussed, what difference does any of this make to your life today? Three facts may help.

1. Interpretive approaches must not divide fellowship.

We can agree on the essentials of the Christian faith while disagreeing about this speculative theological area.

We should always interpret the Bible according to its intended meaning. Scripture can never mean what it never meant. If a suggested interpretation would hold little or no relevance or meaning for the original audience of God's word, it is suspect for us as well.

2. We must be ready to meet the Lord whenever he comes.

He may come for us today, or we may go to him. Our earthly lives may end in physical death or Jesus' return, but we will all one day stand before his throne (2 Corinthians 5:10). And we have only today to be ready. "Tomorrow" is promised nowhere in God's word. So live every day as if it were your last because one day you'll be right.

3. We must be witnesses to prepare others for Jesus' return.

Why, then, does the second coming matter? Jesus makes clear the practical response to our perennial question: "You will be my witnesses." The Bible is not a speculative book. We ask rational, philosophical questions. We want to know about creation and the end times, two subjects about which we can do nothing. But God's word was not written in the western, Greek, rational tradition. It is a Hebrew book, written from the Hebrew present-tense, practical world view. It seldom tells us all we want to know, but it always tells us what we need to know in order to accomplish God's purpose for our lives.

And it is clear: "You will be my witnesses." No one knows when Jesus will return, so everyone must be ready. You and I must be ready. Then we must help other people be ready.

And we are promised only today to do so. The early Christians understood this, so they lived in the daily expectation of Jesus' imminent return. They wanted to be found doing what they would be doing if they knew Jesus were coming back that day. They wanted everyone they knew to be right with God, and they had a passion for missions and evangelism because they knew the time was short.

They were right. Jesus may come back for us all today. Or you and I may go to him.

Either way, the time is short.

Consider the word of God:

- "Besides this you know the time, that the hour has come for you to wake from sleep. For salvation is nearer to us now than when we first believed. The night is far gone; the day is at hand. So then let us cast off the works of darkness and put on the armor of light. Let us walk properly as in the daytime" (Romans 13:11–13).

  Are you living in the "daytime"?

- "Since all these things are thus to be dissolved, what sort of people ought you to be in lives of holiness and godliness, waiting for and hastening the coming of the day of God" (2 Peter 3:11–12).

  Are you looking forward to his return?

- "We must work the works of him who sent me while it is day; night is coming, when no one can work" (John 9:4).

  Are you doing his works while you can?

- "And now, little children, abide in him, so that when he appears we may have confidence and not shrink from him in shame at his coming" (1 John 2:28).

  If it were today, would you "have confidence at his coming"?

- "Behold, I am coming like a thief! Blessed is the one who stays awake, keeping his garments on, that he may not go about naked and be seen exposed!" (Revelation 16:15).

  Are you awake? Are you ready?

- "Behold, I am coming soon, bringing my recompense with me, to repay each one for what he has done" (Revelation 22:12).

If right now you're thinking, "I have plenty of time, this doesn't apply to me," know that you are deceived and wrong.

DON'T WAIT

Perhaps you've heard the old story about the time the devil had a meeting of his demons to decide how best to deceive men and women.

One said, "Let's tell them there's no heaven," but the devil said that wouldn't work, that God has put heaven in every heart and we know it's real.

Another said, "Let's tell them there's no hell," but the devil said that people know wrong must be punished, so that won't work.

Finally a third said, "Let's tell them there's no hurry."

And they did.

And they still do.

So I must ask you, are you ready to see him? If it were today, would you mourn or rejoice?

Are there conversations you'd regret not having? People with whom you would have shared the good news of Jesus?

If you knew he were coming back today, what would you change in your life?

Dwight Moody presented the gospel one Sunday, then told his vast congregation to go home and think about it. The next Sunday he would give an invitation, and he would expect them to come to Jesus.

But that night the Great Chicago Fire began.

Eighteen *thousand* buildings were destroyed; $200 million was lost, a third of the entire city's value. No one knows how many died, but some estimates range as high as fifteen thousand casualties, many of whom had been in Moody's service.

He never waited again.

Nor should we.

A DISCUSSION GUIDE ON THE RAPTURE

1. Before reading this chapter, what came to mind when you thought about the rapture? In what ways, if any, has your view changed after reading?

2. Does looking at the passages in 1 Thessalonians 4 and 5 through the lens of pastoral ministry impact the way you think about them eschatologically?

3. Given the arguments for and against the rapture, which do you find most convincing? Why?

4. Given the arguments for and against Christians facing the tribulation, which do you find most convincing? Why?

5. What are some practical ways we can have conversations about the end times that foster a closer sense of community among Christians rather than fostering division?

6. What is one thing you can do today to better prepare for either Christ coming back or you going to Christ?

3

DEFENDING YOURSELF WITHOUT ATTACKING YOUR WITNESS

What does the Bible say about self-defense and gun control?

Since the beginning of 2022, America has averaged around 1.5 shootings every day where four or more people were injured or killed. A recent study revealed that guns killed more young people than car accidents in 2020 and 2021. On the other hand, millions of Americans own guns responsibly. There are multiple reasons to own firearms (e.g., target shooting, hunting, etc.), but the most common justification is self-defense.

However, some Christians advocate for strict nonviolence, or pacifism. They interpret the teachings and example of Jesus to mean Christians should never engage in violence, even to defend themselves or others.

While a great deal of debate also surrounds whether Christians should serve in the military and whether war is ever justified, that is not the focus of this chapter. For now, we'll look at what the Bible says about self-defense and whether Christians can ever use force in that context. As part of that conversation, we will also discuss gun control from a Christian point of view.

WHAT DOES THE BIBLE SAY ABOUT SELF-DEFENSE?

Let's begin by looking at the most commonly used Bible passages in the debate over self-defense.

Luke 22:36–37: Sell your cloak to buy a sword

At this point in Luke's gospel, Jesus is meeting with his disciples in the "upper room" and is about to go to his death on the cross. Before they leave the Passover dinner, he explains that a new season of ministry will arrive. Instead of wandering from town to town without any possessions, he tells the disciples to carry a knapsack and money bag and to "let the one who has no sword sell his cloak and buy one" (Luke 22:35–38).

Many believe that he is urging his disciples to buy a sword for protection since traveling will become more perilous. On the other hand, some commentators say Jesus does not mean this command literally. Perhaps he's referring to a "spiritual" sword of some kind, although it's hard to see why Jesus would urge them to sell their cloak to buy a spiritual sword.

Alternatively, Malcolm O. Tolbert writes, "Jesus' statement . . . must be a way of emphasizing that the disciples are about to enter a time of great peril—a point that apparently was lost on them." It is as though Jesus is saying, "Boy, you're going to *wish* you had a sword!" While this interpretation seems possible, it is perhaps not the most likely.

Normally, looking at the context helps us understand the intention behind Christ's words. However, in this case, it just makes his saying even more confusing. Jesus continues: "'For I tell you that this Scripture must be fulfilled in me: "And he was numbered with the transgressors." For what is written about me has its fulfillment.' And they said, 'Look, Lord, here are two swords.' And he said to them, 'It is enough.'" (Luke 22:37–38)

The phrase "It is enough" is tricky to translate. Some scholars take it to mean Jesus is rebuking them—basically yelling "Enough!" Obviously, the two swords were not "enough" to fight off the mob about to arrest Jesus. And, in just a few verses he will discourage Peter from using the sword. (We'll discuss that passage in a moment).

So, it doesn't seem clear what Jesus is saying. The most likely explanation is that he is suggesting, in a general way, that in the next season of ministry, the disciples will want to get swords for protection. Basically, they should return to more sustainable ways of doing ministry, and this includes owning a sword. And when Jesus says, "It is enough," he probably means that the two swords are enough for him to be "numbered among the transgressors" when he is arrested.

The coming events would confirm Jesus' use of Isaiah's prophecy. Peter will "transgress" by cutting off the ear of Malchus, who was part of the mob that came to arrest Jesus, presumably using one of those two swords. This fact shows that Jesus is in complete control on the night of his death.

Regardless, because we *could* reasonably take his saying as metaphorical, let's continue with other verses.

Matthew 26:51–56: Sheath your sword

After Peter cuts off the servant of the high priest's ear, Jesus responds, "Put your sword back into its place. For all who take the sword will perish by the sword. Do you think that I cannot appeal to my Father, and he will at once send me more than twelve legions of angels? But how then should the Scriptures be fulfilled, that it must be so?" (Matthew 26:52–54). Jesus goes on to heal the man's ear before the mob takes him away to face condemnation.

"For all who take the sword will perish by the sword" is likely a paraphrase of Jeremiah 15:2. Christian pacifists use this verse to refer to "an absolutely universal principle," arguing that this means Christians must never engage in violence. In their view, although it *seems* like using force can save lives, in the end, violence is never the correct response.

However, it's better to interpret this saying as a general "observation that violence breeds violence." In other words, it's more proverbial than a moral absolute. Jesus saying this makes perfect sense given the situation.

Through his crucifixion, Jesus is about to show that suffering injustice and sacrificing yourself for your enemies is more admirable than responding with violence. At this moment, Jesus is in the profound, divinely planned act of laying down his life to pay for the sins of humanity. Peter's rash attack will not stop God's divine plan. Practically speaking, they could not have stopped the mob with only two swords anyway. If Jesus had wanted to lead a messianic revolt against the Roman army or protect himself from the mob, he could have called tens of thousands of angels to his aid.

However, Jesus' general statement does not necessarily and universally ban using force to protect oneself or others. In this instance, Peter's foolish violence would only have led to a worse outcome, so Jesus rebukes Peter. Jesus is also showing that his kingdom will not come through violent insurrection, a truth that remains unchanged even today. Though history is filled with far too many examples of the church forgetting Christ's prohibition against expanding his kingdom at the tip of a sword, it remains essential for us to remember that we are not to bring God's kingdom to earth through violence of any kind.

Yet, there is an important distinction between a prohibition against violence as a means of evangelism and violence in the defense of oneself or others. To that end, let's look at another of Christ's teachings on the subject.

Matthew 5:9: "Blessed are the peacemakers"

In this verse of the Beatitudes, Jesus encourages his followers to be "peacemakers." That phrase includes not only those who "keep the peace," but those who actively "seek to bring men into harmony with each other." Christians should be the kind of people who bring Jesus' kingdom to earth by making peace wherever they can.

This kingdom of God will not be fully sealed until the Day of Judgment, but we can start bringing it to earth by living as citizens of God's kingdom. God's kingdom will ultimately be one of peace, as described in Isaiah 9:6–7, 66:12–13, and Micah 4:3. It is the ultimate ideal for all Christians, and creating peace wherever we go is certainly one of our primary roles in this life.

However, this again does not seem to universally negate the use of force in every situation. For example, Jesus turns over tables in righteous anger in the Temple, divinely enraged at the extortion happening in his Father's house (Matthew 21:12). Few of those manning those tables would have considered this action peaceful. Yet, this rare, sinless display of righteous anger did bring about a more peaceful resolution as it cleared the Temple for Jesus to heal the blind and the lame while ministering to all those who came near (Matthew 21:14).

Yet, we are not Jesus, and his actions here are not meant to serve as a template for how we should address acts of sin and corruption. Rather, his call to us is to be peacemakers, and the use of violence to that end should be the exception rather than the rule and only undertaken as a last resort.

Matthew 5:39: "Turn the other cheek"

Another passage to which Christian pacifists frequently appeal is Matthew 5:39. From it, they argue that we must suffer violence and never return it. Certainly, this verse is a core teaching of love and aligns with how Christ lived, so let's unpack it more.

One commentator summarizes this section, "A righteous man would be characterized by humility and selflessness . . . he might go 'the extra mile' to maintain peace. When wronged . . . he would not strike back, demand repayment, or refuse to comply. Instead of retaliating he would do the opposite, and would also commit his case to the Lord who will one day set all things in order."

But does this mean that, universally, we can never defend ourselves or others? It does not.

First, note that this passage is part of a series of examples where Jesus calls his followers to give up their rights in order to earn the opportunity to enhance their witness. Each instance occurs within a context where it is clear his disciples have the right to act otherwise. As such, even if Christ was calling us not to defend ourselves—more on that shortly—it is also evident that we have the right to do so.

Second, as Craig Blomberg writes, "Striking a person on the right cheek suggests a backhanded slap from a typically right-handed aggressor and was a characteristic Jewish form of insult. Jesus tells us not to trade such insults even if it means receiving more. In no sense does v. 39 require Christians to subject themselves or others to physical danger or abuse, nor does it bear directly on the pacifism" debate.

If we take it at the extreme to mean that Jesus commands all Christians to passively allow violence to be done to them, think of the abusive situations in which his people would be trapped. It's also inconsistent with Jesus' actions, who at one point used his divine power to escape violent crowds (Luke 4:29–30). Pacifists allow for running away from violence (and that seems to nearly always be the right option), but it seems to me that *if* we take Jesus' statement as referring to violence, we would need to simply accept violence done to us.

A more accurate interpretation of this passage teaches us that we should de-escalate situations as much as possible, acting as peacemakers. And Jesus' teaching certainly prohibits the use of force or insult in retaliation, anger, or revenge. However, these principles do not seem to prohibit using force to guard our safety and the safety of others.

Exodus 22:2–3: The killing of a "thief found breaking in"

In the Old Testament, God gave the Israelites laws that showed his just character and desire for order. The first five books of the Bible are called "Torah," which means "teaching," or "instruction." So, even though the Levitical laws don't always apply directly to God's people anymore, we should still learn important lessons from them.

In Exodus, one of the laws for Israel states, "If a thief is found breaking in and is struck so that he dies, there shall be no bloodguilt for him, but if the sun has risen on him, there shall be bloodguilt for him" (Exodus 22:2–3)

There are a couple of key ideas in this text. First, if there is a home invader at night who is presumably stealing from you and you kill them while defending your home, you are not guilty of murder. The second is harder to nail down: Why is it different in the daytime?

There are a few explanations. First, the thief could be more easily caught during the day. Another suggestion is that if the thief is stealing during the daytime, he is less likely to kill someone. At night, it seems more likely that someone entering your house is intruding and up to no good, whereas in the day, they might be doing something odd but not wrong. Or, maybe the difference is that a groggy person awoken at night may not reasonably be able to hold back how forceful they are.

In any case, the goal of the homeowner is clearly to deter the robber or have the authorities capture them and bring them to justice. In the next verse, the Bible lays out the just, corresponding punishment: The thief will either pay the amount back or be sold into slavery (v. 4).

The biblical laws give protection even to criminals. And while, today, we do not always keep to the consequences they proscribe, it's important to recognize that they "did not allow unlimited freedom to the victim of a crime to defend or retaliate." While capital punishment was sometimes mentioned in the Old Testament, it is notable that even thieves possess the image of God. Each person, even a criminal, is a human being with inherent worth.

This passage clearly means an individual cannot kill a criminal in revenge or in service of vigilante justice. It also suggests that even if you are defending your house, you shouldn't *intend* to kill the thief.

The passage in Exodus gives the impression that we should try to repel home invaders and bring them to justice through due process. If, in the confusion of the moment, we kill the invader in defense, we are not guilty of murder. But, if we kill them knowing there is no threat to us, we *do* commit murder, even if they've wronged us. As such, this passage seems to support self-defense while also creating strict limits on when to use it and where to draw the line.

Romans 12:18–19: "If possible . . . live peaceably with all"

The final passage we'll look at for this chapter offers a fitting conclusion to our discussion about the Bible's teachings on self-defense: "If possible, so far as it depends on you, live peaceably with all. Beloved, never avenge yourselves, but leave it to the wrath of God, for it is written, 'Vengeance is mine, I will repay, says the Lord.' To the contrary, 'if your enemy is hungry, feed him; if he is thirsty, give him something to drink; for by so doing you will heap burning coals on his head.' Do not be overcome by evil, but overcome evil with good" (Romans 12:18–19).

This has a wide range of applications. If a neighbor steals from you, use Spirit-inspired discretion, leaning on the side of love—answering evil with good. If *at all possible*, live peaceably with people, even criminals. However, Paul recognizes it's not possible in this broken, fallen world to live peaceably with everyone. But that is still a tall order, and we should not neglect it: in every area of our lives, we must live peaceably with *everyone*, by every possible means In other places, Paul appeals to Roman law to protect himself (Acts 22:22–23; 25:10). Other times, he rejoices in his own suffering and persecution (Romans 5:3).

Theologian Robert H. Mounce summarizes this well: "The natural impulse is to return injury for injury. But retaliation for personal injury is not for those who claim to follow the one who told his disciples to turn the other cheek and go the second mile (Matt 5:39, 41; cf. Gal 6:10; 1 Thess 5:15; 1 Pet 3:9). Instead, believers are to be careful to do what is honorable in the sight of everyone."

Using force to protect life

Just as we should submit to the governing authorities *unless* they command us to do something against God's will, we should show sacrificial love—even to our enemies—*unless* we have no other choice in order to protect others or ourselves.

Violence should be treated as our last possible resort in defending ourselves or our families. And even in that case, we must try to avoid killing the attacker or invader if at all possible. We must never use force in revenge or anger, vigilantism, or spite. God will hold all sins accountable: the sins of the criminal and our own sins as well.

Moreover, the argument can be made that the bar for when to use violence should be set even higher if you are only defending yourself. If it looks like an intruder intends to harm your family, that's a time to use force. If you are the only one there, trying to defuse the situation through nonviolent means is the best route. Or even cooperating with the criminal can be a better alternative to violence in some cases. Of course, we are *allowed* to defend ourselves, but the ultimate goal is for everyone to leave the situation alive.

We should all long for the day when the kingdom of God is brought to earth in its fullest sense. When we will "beat [our] plowshares into swords, and [our] pruning hooks into spears" (Joel 3:10).

The position of pacifism is understandable. We long to be free from violence and hatred and even the potential need to defend ourselves. Jesus' life on earth gives, arguably, the biggest argument in favor of pacifism. He exercised nonviolence throughout his ministry in surprising ways.

And yet, though we long to be free from violence, sometimes in the interest of protecting life, force is warranted.

SHOULD CHRISTIANS DEFEND THEMSELVES?

Pacifists mostly rest their case on the example of Jesus. The draw of following Jesus in an entirely nonviolent way, always turning the other cheek, is understandable. The conversation gets a bit tricky, however, when it comes to the case of persecution for our faith.

In history, Christians often sought to escape from persecution. Other times, they accepted violence done to them without resistance. For example, Stephen, imitating

Christ, looked up to heaven and, as his last act on earth, forgave those who were killing him (Acts 6:8–8:1). Paul (the man who approved Stephen's execution) at times faced persecution without flinching (Acts 21:27–40) and, at others, sought to escape it (Acts 9:23–25).

So, we have examples to avoid persecution, either through the law or by fleeing. However, we don't have any examples of self-defense in the face of persecution. It seems like Christians should not fight back with force if we are being persecuted explicitly *because of* our faith. We may also be able to defend our families from persecution with force, although that exception isn't clear. The main thrust here is that Christianity itself should not become associated with violence.

So, while the Bible seems to permit using force in personal self-defense and to prevent further violence, it seems to show that Christians should take a nonviolent stance when confronted by persecution. Ultimately, however, it calls us to go to God with these decisions and follow his will. It may be that he would have you respond in different ways depending on the context, so do not become so legalistic that you presume to know his will before you ask.

The Bible speaks with greater clarity, however, in its call to live peaceably wherever possible. We must be *known* as bringers of peace. Using force is the rare exception. We should not "fetishize" guns or violence. We do not enforce Christian teaching with violence. And we do not convert people by threatening them. We point people to Jesus with our loving, unifying actions. But, in this broken world, when the need arises to protect ourselves or to deter further violence, we are permitted to use force.

With that understanding in mind, let's conclude the chapter by turning to one of the more divisive applications of this discussion: gun control.

HOW SHOULD CHRISTIANS CONSIDER GUN CONTROL?

Most Americans' opinions on gun control sit on a spectrum. Americans are usually not for banning all guns, and most don't affirm unrestricted access. At the most basic level, advocates for stricter gun legislation value safety. While those who defend gun rights typically prioritize freedom above other values, they also value safety. The number one reason cited for legally owning a gun is self-protection.

Gun rights activists claim that human behavior is the issue at the root of gun violence, not guns. They will often support stricter policing coupled with fewer gun restrictions.

Gun control activists say that guns make a variety of situations more deadly, especially certain kinds of guns, and that more guns in a system mean the wrong people will get them.

Both can make valid and defensible arguments, but which side most closely aligns with Scripture? The answer—like issues of self-defense in general—tends to get complicated quickly. And one of the main reasons is that both sides tend to use the same terms but with different definitions.

Take assault rifles, for example. People in favor of greater gun control tend to support laws banning assault rifles. Yet, for the most part, that's already happened. The US has heavily restricted what our military calls assault rifles, which refers to a rifle with the ability to toggle between fully automatic and semi-automatic firing. On the other hand, some semi-automatic weapons were included in the assault weapon ban of 1994, a law that has since expired.

When the media talks about assault rifles, they typically mean semi-automatic rifles. Semi-automatic refers to a gun that shoots once every time you pull the trigger without the user needing to cock the gun. Yet, in recent years such rifles have accounted for roughly 3 percent of firearm murders, whereas handguns made up 59 percent.

On the other hand, semi-automatic rifles were used in many *mass shootings,* another term to be wary of because its definition varies widely. Typically, a mass shooting refers to four people killed or injured (besides the shooter) at the same event. Some researchers also qualify that it must be "indiscriminate," meaning it excludes gang violence, armed robbery, or domestic violence.

Depending on how these definitions are used, the statistics can vary widely. In 2019, for example, there were either six mass shootings or up to five hundred. This is because gang violence and domestic violence are included in the five hundred number, whereas the six only included shooters who weren't targeting anyone in particular, such as with most school shootings.

Both categories are tragic, but much of the difficulty in having productive conversations about this topic is due more to disagreement on terminology than attempts to deceive. There's a deeper layer of awareness about terms that's needed when talking about policy issues, not only with regard to guns themselves but also with regard to the way studies use statistics in general. And, given that proponents on both sides of the issue often point to statistics to defend their argument, understanding what those numbers mean is crucial to having an informed discussion.

THE TRAGIC "INVISIBLE" STATISTIC IN THE GUN CONTROL DEBATE

According to the CDC in 2021, 54 percent of gun deaths were caused by suicide, and 43 percent were due to murder of some kind. The remaining 3 percent were unintentional, involved law enforcement, or took place under unidentified circumstances. The total number of gun deaths in 2021 was 48,830.

However, those numbers represented a shift in what had been a long-declining trajectory. 2021's figures, for example, represented a 23 percent increase over 2019. Moreover, there were 14.6 gun deaths per 100,000 people in 2021. And while that was the highest rate since the mid-1990s, it remained far below the statistic's peak of 16.3 in 1974.

Fortunately, it looks like those trends may be starting to reverse, with the total number of gun deaths in 2023 dropping to 42,373. What has not changed, however, is that suicide remains the primary cause of gun deaths in America.

We've written more extensively about suicide in a chapter dedicated to the subject. Yet, we highlight its role here because when most people think of gun violence, they typically go first to stories of mass shootings, murder, and domestic violence. Suicide, by contrast, tends to get lost in the conversation when it should be a crucial component in where we go from here. As such, it offers a tragically fitting reminder of the way that people often allow their perceptions rather than reality to define their views on the subject of self-defense in general and gun control in particular.

So, as we finish our discussion on this subject, let's conclude with two practical applications that should help direct not only our views but how we approach sharing them with others.

TWO PRACTICAL APPLICATIONS

First, remember that the goal of self-defense in every situation should be to save lives.

The Bible teaches that life is sacred from conception to death and that each person is made in God's image (Genesis 1:27). As Christians, we are called to treat every person we meet as someone who is loved and valued by God while seeing death—particularly when it comes through violent means—as an outcome to be avoided wherever possible.

It's easy to dismiss the deaths of criminals as negligible or suicides as unavoidable. While it is true that earthly governments should wield the sword for justice, even the life of the criminal is sacred (Romans 13:3–4). That doesn't mean it's always wrong to kill—although it is always wrong to murder (Exodus 20:13)—but it does mean that we should prize and value life above essentially all else.

Accidental deaths, suicides, gang-related killings, domestic homicides, and mass shootings are all part of the massive number of gun-related deaths every year and drive much of the conversation behind the larger discussion on self-defense as well. Whatever the solution to each of these separate issues, we must remember that *all* life is sacred and should be protected where possible.

Second, the full scope of these issues can be difficult to grasp while the evidence, dozens of scientific studies, and countless terms are often befuddling. Each of us should remember to listen carefully, not be quick to anger, and humble ourselves, knowing that our knowledge is limited and our perspectives are often influenced by experiences and contexts we may not fully understand (Proverbs 15:1; 19:1; James 1:19; Ephesians 4:31).

Remember that Jesus has called us to be peacemakers, and that becomes much more difficult to accomplish if we are so committed to one perspective that we cannot at least consider other views as well. Those who think differently than us are not the enemy, and to treat them as such undermines not only our ability to have a productive conversation on issues of self-defense but our ability to share the gospel as well.

God has not called us to be evangelists for pacifism, gun lobbies, or any of the other perspectives that often speak with such conviction on these issues. However, he has called us to be evangelists for Jesus, and anything that gets in the way of that effort is necessarily outside of his will for our lives.

So the next time you get the opportunity to discuss this topic, remember to engage in the conversation with God's larger perspective in mind. These issues are important and worthy of both prayer and reflection, but they pale in comparison to the importance of the gospel.

Let's be sure our approach to them reflects that reality.

A DISCUSSION GUIDE ON SELF-DEFENSE AND GUN CONTROL

1. Of the passages examined in this chapter regarding self-defense, is there one that stands out as giving the clearest instruction on this issue?

2. In what instances, if any, do you think the Bible allows for the use of force?

3. To what extent should there be a difference between the use of force being permissible and the use of force being the best course of action?

4. How has disagreement on terms made the issue of gun control more difficult to discuss? Can you think of any other subjects where this same problem of relying on different definitions for the same terms has created issues?

5. What was your initial reaction upon learning that suicide was the primary cause of gun deaths in America? Does that impact the way you see the broader issue of gun control?

6. When you think about violence, does the death of a criminal seem less tragic than the death of a non-criminal? Should they be viewed differently? Why or why not?

7. How can we engage with this subject in ways that enhance our witness and ability to share the gospel?

4

"THE GLEAMING FUTURISTIC LAND OF OZ"

What does the Bible say about artificial intelligence?

"This is going to change *everything* about how we do *everything*. I think that it represents mankind's greatest invention to date. It is qualitatively different—and it will be transformational" (his italics). This is how Craig Mundie, former chief research and strategy officer for Microsoft, described GPT-4 to *New York Times* columnist Thomas Friedman.

After seeing a demonstration of this technology, Friedman recalled the tornado scene in *The Wizard of Oz* when everything is "swept away from mundane, black and white Kansas to the gleaming futuristic Land of Oz, where everything is in color." He then observed: "We are about to be hit by such a tornado."

Friedman explained: "This is a Promethean moment we've entered—one of those moments in history when certain new tools, ways of thinking or energy sources are introduced that are such a departure and advance on what existed before that you can't just change one thing, you have to change everything. That is, how you create, how you compete, how you collaborate, how you work, how you learn, how you govern and, yes, how you cheat, commit crimes, and fight wars."

He listed "key Promethean eras" of the last six centuries: the invention of the printing press, the scientific revolution, the agricultural revolution combined with the industrial revolution, the nuclear power revolution, and personal computing and the internet. Then he stated that **artificial intelligence** (AI) is another such moment.

He writes: "The potential to use these tools to solve seemingly impossible problems—from human biology to fusion energy to climate change—is awe-inspiring." But he warns that AI is "dual use": it can be a tool or a weapon with cataclysmic consequences for good or evil.

Also, please note: Progress in the field of AI moves rapidly, which is one reason why it offers both hope and hesitation. While everything that follows is up to date at the time of writing, the pace of innovation means that some of the information discussed below may have changed by the time you read it.

WHAT IS ARTIFICIAL INTELLIGENCE?

The term *artificial intelligence* was coined in the late 1950s by a group of academics who set out to build a machine that could do anything the human brain could do. This would include skills such as reasoning, problem-solving, learning new tasks, and communicating using natural language.

Progress continued slowly until 2012, when an idea called the **neural network** shifted the entire field. This is a mathematical system that learns skills by finding statistical patterns in enormous amounts of data. For example, such a system can learn to recognize a cat by analyzing thousands of cat photos. This is how Siri and Alexa understand what you're saying, how Google Photos identifies people and objects, and how apps can instantly translate dozens of languages.

The next big step came around 2018 with **large language models** (LLM). Companies such as Google, Microsoft, and OpenAI began building neural networks trained on vast amounts of text including digital books, academic papers, and Wikipedia articles. Surprisingly, these systems learned to write unique prose and computer code and to carry on sophisticated conversations. This step is sometimes called **generative AI** because the AI can generate output via text, code, imagery, or video.

WHAT ARE CHATBOTS LIKE CHATGPT?

As a result, ChatGPT and other "chatbots" are "now poised to change our everyday lives in dramatic ways."

GPT stands for **generative pre-trained transformer**, which is "a program that can realistically write like a human." It was developed by OpenAI, a San Francisco-based AI firm founded by leaders in the tech industry, with notable names Elon Musk and Sam Altman as initial board members. Its primary goal is to "generate human-like texts based on the input provided by the user." When users input a sentence or question to the model, GPT processes the query and generates information by extracting it from the dataset available to it.

GPT-4, the latest version, was launched in March 2023. It allows users to provide input in text and image forms. It has produced human-like performances on several academic and professional benchmarks and has even passed the bar exam and LSAT.

English computer scientist Stephen Wolfram explains that "what ChatGPT is always fundamentally trying to do is produce a 'reasonable continuation' of whatever text it's got so far, where by 'reasonable' we mean 'what one might expect someone to write after seeing what people have written on billions of webpages, etc.'"

His article explains ChatGPT in great depth, but it can be summarized as follows:

- ChatGPT completes sentences and answers queries by building sentences word by word based on statistical probabilities. It is essentially asking over and over again, "Given the text so far, what should the next word be?"

- It develops these probabilities from its expansive knowledge base.

- It utilizes "neural nets" by which it processes billions of numeric computations to generalize from particular examples to "reason" to logical responses.

OpenAI has now allowed ChatGPT to access the internet, run its own code to solve problems, accept and work on uploaded files, and write its own interfaces to third-party apps.

WHAT CAN ARTIFICIAL INTELLIGENCE DO?

So where are we likely to go from here?

Google Assistant, Apple Siri, Be My Eyes, and others are using GPT to improve their language abilities and provide human-like responses that are surprisingly accurate and relevant when the prompts are simple. They help users manage tasks such as scheduling meetings, planning the day, reminding of tasks, and more. GPT language models are being used by Uber and others to provide faster answers and help access maximum productivity in customer service.

Major companies are also using GPT to develop content for their web pages, social media channels, blogs, articles, and more. They can generate content at a faster pace and improve the overall quality and unique ideas for their content as a result. Such content can be optimized for SEO, helping to gain maximum webpage traffic.

Bill Gates predicts that AI will enable health workers to be more productive with paperwork, notes, and insurance claims. It will enable patients to do basic triage, get advice for medical problems, and decide whether they need to seek treatment. And it will "dramatically accelerate the rate of medical breakthroughs" as it mines the immense amount of data available to it.

For example, the UCSF Cell Design Institute and the IBM Almaden Research Center are working with AI to test different arrangements of T-cells in order to find optimal treatments for cancer patients. Their hope is that altering the receptors in a cell will enable it "to sense the outside environment and provide the cell with instructions on how to respond to environmental conditions."

Essentially, they're teaching cells to identify cancer and kill it without having to resort to chemotherapy, radiation, or the host of other treatments that often do as much damage to the patient as to the disease.

While there is still a long way to go, the techniques are promising. Moreover, AI can empower the sharing of data and outcomes around the world as well.

The work of cardiologist James Min is one such example. He has produced "Cleerly," an AI-based evaluation system that scans the heart and was found to have an overall accuracy rate of 84 percent. This technology analyzes the arteries of the heart to predict the likelihood that plaque buildup may lead to a future heart attack. It can also detect early signs of heart disease. Physicians can then use this information to create an individualized treatment plan for their patients. Min's ultimate goal for Cleerly is a "heart-attack free" world.

Gates thinks AI-driven software will also personalize learning, assist teachers and administrators, and make education available to more people than ever.

Sam Altman, the co-founder of OpenAI, told an interviewer, "What I am personally most excited about is helping us greatly expand our scientific knowledge. I am a believer that a lot of our forward progress comes from increasing scientific discovery over a long period of time."

He added, "This is going to elevate humanity in ways we still can't fully envision. And our children, our children's children, are going to be far better off than the best of anyone from this time. And we're just going to be in a radically improved world. We will live healthier, more interesting, more fulfilling lives."

Or at least that's the goal.

As we continue to progress further down the path of improving AI, however, those who are working most closely with the latest developments are often the ones who can seem the most nervous about where we're heading.

WHAT ARE THE LIMITATIONS AND DANGERS OF ARTIFICIAL INTELLIGENCE?

GPT is trained in using statistical patterns of language. As a result, it cannot always understand a user's context and might generate technically valid responses without broader context in the real world.

Currently, it also contains only limited long-term memory, so it might struggle to maintain consistency in texts or during chats. And while it lacks emotion and empathy, it is abounding in confidence. Even incorrect answers are offered with little hint that they could be wrong, making it difficult to know when AI functions as a reliable source of information and when it could be misleading.

As Cade Metz of the *New York Times* describes, "AI is not as powerful as it might seem. If you take a step back, you realize that these systems can't duplicate our common sense or reasoning in full. Remember the hype around self-driving cars: Were those cars impressive?

Yes, remarkably so. Were they ready to replace human drivers? Not by a long shot."

However, Kevin Roose replied, "I suspect that tools like ChatGPT are actually *more* powerful than they seem. We haven't yet discovered everything they can do. And, at the risk of getting too existential, I'm not sure these models work so differently than our brains. Isn't a lot of human reasoning just recognizing patterns and predicting what comes next?" (his italics).

Gates is especially concerned with "the possibility that AIs will run out of control." He asks, "Could a machine decide that humans are a threat, conclude that its interests are different from ours, or simply stop caring about us?"

He adds that "superintelligent AIs are in our future" and that they "will be able to do everything that a human brain can, but without any practical limits on the size of its memory or the speed at which it operates." However, these "strong AIs" will "probably be able to establish their own goals."

He asks, "What will these goals be? What happens if they conflict with humanity's interests? Should we try to prevent strong AI from ever being developed?" He adds, "These questions will get more pressing with time."

The late physicist Stephen Hawking said, "AI could develop a will of its own, a will that is in conflict with ours and which could destroy us." Elon Musk similarly warned, "Artificial intelligence is a fundamental risk to human civilization."

As such, two camps have developed in response to these growing fears, though it's unclear which will win out in the end.

WHO WILL ULTIMATELY CONTROL AI?

The first camp wants to slow down, thinking the best way to protect against AI going too far is to put safeguards around its development.

This perspective is understandable, and President Biden's executive order in late 2023 was intended largely to establish such guardrails. Even the aforementioned Elon Musk joined more than a thousand experts in the field to call for a pause in any further development while the industry tries to catch up to the massive leaps that have happened across recent years. Their hope is that we can get to a place where the technology does not outpace our ability to control it.

The example of social media has come up as a frequent warning as it often feels like damage control is the best we can hope for in response to its vastly increased influence within the culture. The fear is that, should artificial intelligence get similarly out of hand, the consequences would be far more dire.

Ultimately, this perspective is understandable, and there is certainly a degree of wisdom to taking a step back to evaluate what should come next. The problem is that for such a pause to work, everyone in the field would have to agree to it. Given the massive wealth and opportunities that come with being at the forefront of development, counting on everyone playing by the rules is naïve at best. As a result, a second camp appears likely to carry the day going forward.

Most in the field recognize the dangers of artificial intelligence developing too quickly. But those who recognize the futility of trying to slow that progress argue that the best way to guard against the worst outcomes is to make sure the most responsible parties are the ones driving that innovation. They argue that taking a step back will simply allow less trustworthy groups to catch up and then take the lead in where AI goes from here.

As Michael Frank of the Center for Strategic and International Studies warns, "There will be AI. And so if that's the case, then you want the people who care about developing safe AI" to get there first. Frank goes on to add that many in this camp believe they "have a responsibility to be the first one[s] so that [they] can shape the future of AI."

And though it's understandable—and reasonable— if your initial reaction to that logic is a strong mix of skepticism and cynicism, that doesn't make their argument wrong either. Given the way that technology has already become a primary battlefield for global conflicts, AI is likely to play a defining role in how nations engage with one another going forward. The potential advantages are simply too great to expect that any will set them aside for the greater good of all humanity.

So if artificial intelligence is going to keep progressing regardless of the inherent risks and there is little that can be done to slow it down, where does that leave us?

"FOR SUCH A TIME AS THIS"

In *Who Will Rule the Coming 'Gods'? The Looming Spiritual Crisis of Artificial Intelligence*, Wallace B. Henley issued a warning to our postmodern, post-Christian culture. Henley is a former White House and congressional aide who has been a journalist and a teaching pastor.

When a friend warned him of the dangers of AI, Henley writes, "I suddenly became aware of how vulnerable humanity will be as the machines seem increasingly godlike in an age when people are rejecting beliefs in God as the Transcendent Being to whom all are accountable and giving the contraptions of their own making an almost godlike power and position."

He asks, "Who or what will control all of this? To what values and worldviews will the machines be programmed to submit? In the final analysis, will they obey their human masters, or will human beings become the mastered?"

Ultimately, we can't know the answer to those questions.

And while that uncertainty can be vexing, we must not let the worries of the future become more important than the concerns of the present. After all, Christ's instruction nearly two thousand years ago remains as relevant today as it was back then: "Do not be anxious about tomorrow, for tomorrow will be anxious for itself. Sufficient for the day is its own trouble" (Matthew 6:34).

Instead, let's keep our focus on what the Lord has called us to do today and remember that we serve a God who is greater than any humans could ever create.

While AI has access to current digital data, God is so omniscient that he knows the past, present, future, and the thoughts of every human heart (Matthew 12:25). AI-enabled apps can guide your journey, but Jesus alone can guide you to your best life in this world (John 10:10) and your eternal destination when this life is done (John 14:3).

AI can instruct you; Jesus can forgive you. AI can provide you with information; Jesus can provide you with his loving presence in every valley and storm of life (cf. Matthew 28:20).

This is why knowing Christ and making him known are the most urgent priorities in the world. As Os Guinness notes, "The truth is that our Western commitment to hedonism has proved empty and damaging, and our Western reliance on technocracy will always let us down. Only God can save the world now."

He adds: "Man cannot live by shadows alone. For all who have seen the sun, the shadows will never again deceive and satisfy, but the challenge then is even bigger and more arduous: the task of building societies and a civilization that are genuinely sunlit too."

The good news is that the one true God is still on his throne. None of this surprises him. He has assigned us to this time in human history as missionaries to our culture, with all its challenges and opportunities. He will lead all who will be led as we use the technologies of our day to serve him and advance his kingdom.

Let's pray for the wisdom to use AI as Paul used the Roman roads—to share the good news of God's love with the world. And let's speak biblical truth to the moral issues AI raises as we serve our lost culture with the salt and light of Jesus.

"Who knows whether you have not come to the kingdom for such a time as this?" (Esther 4:14).

A DISCUSSION GUIDE ON ARTIFICIAL INTELLIGENCE

1. Thomas Friedman likened the onset of AI in our culture to a "Promethean moment" that will impact every facet of our lives. Do you think artificial intelligence will have that kind of impact? Why?

2. The quest for artificial intelligence began in the 1950s with the goal of building a machine that could mimic the human brain. In light of what's discussed in this chapter, how has that objective shifted in the decades since?

3. How would you describe your comfort level with AI?

4. Of the two approaches to guarding against artificial intelligence developing beyond our control—slow development or staying at its forefront—which argument do you find most convincing? Why?

5. Can you think of any examples where people you know have made technology—whether AI or in a different form—a replacement for God in their lives? What factors led them to do so?

6. How could AI be used to distance people from the Lord?

7. How could AI be used to advance the kingdom of God today?

5

THE PARDONABLE SIN

What does the Bible say about suicide?

NOTE: If you or someone you know is having thoughts of suicide, please get help immediately. Call or text the 988 Suicide & Crisis Lifeline at 988 or visit 988lifeline.org.

According to the World Health Organization as of 2023, over 700,000 people take their own life every year. Stay Here, a "mental health organization and movement dedicated to ending suicide and healing the broken hearted," says a suicide occurs every forty seconds.

In February 2022, former Miss USA Cheslie Kryst died by suicide. She was by all standards successful. She was a Division-I athlete, won the Miss USA pageant, placed in the top ten Miss Universe competition, and became the host of an entertainment news program *Extra*. She even helped others with her law degree by doing pro bono cases. Tragically, Kryst nonetheless lost herself to suicide, writing that she "only found emptiness" even in her successes. Depression and suicidality can affect even the most successful by the world's standards.

But suicidal thoughts can affect all kinds of people, even pastors. Darrin Patrick, a megachurch pastor, speaker, and author, died by suicide in 2020. According to Seacoast Church, a multi-site megachurch in South Carolina where he was teaching pastor, he died of what appeared to be a "self-inflicted gunshot wound." A longtime friend of Patrick noted that pastors often don't know what to do when they struggle. They attempt to keep up appearances and handle their struggles on their own. "We don't feel like we can ask for help," he said.

As a pastor and a theologian, I am not qualified to offer medical advice or professional counseling to those suffering from anxiety and depression. But I can offer biblical insights on the painful issue of suicide. And let's offer others the hope and help that we find in Christ.

THE SCOPE OF THE ISSUE OF SUICIDE IN AMERICA

More people die from suicide than from homicide in America. According to the Centers for Disease Control and Prevention, suicide rates rose until 2018, increasing 36 percent between 2000 and 2018. It declined a bit until 2020, but it's estimated that since then, they have risen due to the pandemic and the host of other issues that have accompanied it in the years since.

According to the Suicide Prevention Resource Center, suicide is the second-leading cause of death for Americans ages ten to thirty-four. In the UK, it is the leading cause of death among both men and women aged 20–34 and for men through the age of 50. Suicide rates have grown exponentially for women since 1999.

The CDC reports that more than half of the people who died by suicide did not have a known mental health condition.

Factors contributing to suicide include:

- relationship problems
- a crisis in the past or upcoming two weeks
- problematic substance abuse
- physical health problems
- job or financial problems
- criminal or legal problems
- and loss of housing.

There is a direct link between anxiety and opioid use. Those suffering from anxiety are two to three times more likely to have an alcohol or other substance abuse disorder. Anxiety is linked to heart disease, chronic respiratory disorders, and gastrointestinal disorders.

And numerous studies have related anxiety directly to suicide. Compared to those without anxiety, patients with anxiety disorder were more likely to have suicidal ideations, attempted suicides, completed suicides, or suicidal activities.

Anxiety is escalating in our culture. Since the pandemic, over a third of Americans "show symptoms of anxiety, depression, or both." Teens are showing alarming propensities toward suicide. Twenty percent of high school students report serious thoughts of suicide, and nearly ten percent report having attempted suicide, as of 2022.

A recent mental distress survey found that participants were eight times as likely to screen positive for serious mental illness as participants in a similar survey before the pandemic. The vast majority of the 2020 participants, 70 percent, met the criteria for moderate to serious mental illness, showing the detrimental effects of the pandemic isolation. And many have remained in that state across the years since.

These are some of the facts regarding the tragedy of suicide. However, if you are reading this chapter and the subject is more personal than objective for you, I hope the following discussion is helpful.

As I noted, I am writing as a theologian and a minister, not a counselor, psychologist, or psychiatrist. I will offer a brief overview of our subject from a biblical and theological perspective, with some practical suggestions at the conclusion of our conversation.

But if suicide is a real issue for you, I urge you to seek professional help immediately. See the section "Help for those considering suicide" toward the end of this chapter.

THE HISTORY OF SUICIDE

The term *suicide* is traced in the *Oxford English Dictionary* to 1651; its first occurrence is apparently in Sir Thomas Browne's *Religio Medici*, written in 1635 and published in 1642. Before it became a common term, expressions such as "self-murder" and "self-killing" were used to describe the act of taking one's own life.

In Greek and Roman antiquity, suicide was accepted and even seen by some as an honorable means of death and the attainment of immediate salvation. Stoics and others influenced by them saw suicide as the triumph of an individual over fate. Socrates' decision to take his own life rather than violate the state's sentence of execution influenced many to see the act as noble. However, he also made clear that we belong to the gods and cannot end our lives unless they wish it so (Plato, *Phaedo* 62bc).

Many of the early Christians knew they would likely die for their faith but chose to follow Christ at any cost. These deaths are not typically considered "suicide" since they were not initiated by the person but accepted as a consequence of his or her commitment to Jesus.

Augustine (AD 354–430) was a strong opponent of any form of self-murder (cf. *City of God* 1:4–26). He appealed to the sixth commandment and its prohibition against murder. And he agreed with Socrates that our lives belong to God so that we have no right to end them ourselves. Over time, many in the church came to see self-murder as an unpardonable sin (see the discussion of the Catholic Church's position below).

In the nineteenth century, social scientists began to view suicide as a social issue and a symptom of a larger dysfunction in the community and/or home. Medical doctors began to identify depression and other disorders behind the act. Suicide became decriminalized so that the individual could be buried, his family not disinherited, and a survivor not prosecuted.

Many are confused about this difficult subject, as our society and its churches have adopted such a wide variety of positions on it. So, let's discuss biblical teachings on the issue, the Catholic position, a Protestant response, and practical help for those dealing with this tragic problem.

WHAT DOES THE BIBLE SAY ABOUT SUICIDE?

God's word does not use the word *suicide*, but it has much to say on our subject.

Biblical occurrences

The Old Testament records five clear suicides:

1. When Abimelech was mortally wounded by a woman who dropped a millstone on his head, he cried to his armor-bearer to kill him so his death would not be credited to the woman (Judges 9:54).

2. The mortally wounded King Saul fell upon his own sword lest the Philistines abuse him further (1 Samuel 31:4).

3. Saul's armor-bearer then took his own life as well (1 Samuel 31:5).

4. Ahithophel hanged himself after his advice was no longer followed by King David's son Absalom (2 Samuel 17:23).

5. Zimri set himself afire after his rebellion failed (1 Kings 16:18).

Additionally, some consider Jonah to have attempted suicide (Jonah 1:11–15). And Samson destroyed the Philistine temple, killing himself and all those with him (Judges 16:29–30). But many do not see this as a suicide as much as an act of military bravery. The death of Judas is the only clear example of suicide in the New Testament (Matthew 27:3–10). Paul later prevented the suicide of the Philippian jailer and won him to Christ (Acts 16:27–28).

Some consider Jesus' death to have been a kind of suicide since he made clear: "No one takes [my life] from me, but I lay it down of my own accord" (John 10:18). However, as the divine Son of God, he could only have been killed, by any means, with his permission.

Biblical principles

God's word makes clear the sanctity of life:

- "You shall not murder" (Exodus 20:13).

- "This day I call the heavens and the earth as witnesses against you that I have set before you life and death, blessings and curses. Now choose life, so that you and your children may live" (Deuteronomy 30:19).

- "The Lord gave and the Lord has taken away; may the name of the Lord be praised" (Job 1:21).

- "Do you not know that your bodies are temples of the Holy Spirit, who is in you, whom you have received from God? You are not your own; you were bought at a price. Therefore honor God with your bodies" (1 Corinthians 6:19–20).

- "No one ever hated their own body, but they feed and care for their body, just as Christ does the church" (Ephesians 5:29).

There are times when believers may have to give their lives in the service of Christ and his kingdom (cf. Mark 8:34–36; John 13:37; Philippians 1:21–22). But voluntary martyrdom is not usually considered suicide.

As we have seen, our postmodern culture claims that absolute truth does not exist (note that this is an absolute truth claim). In a nontheistic or relativistic society, it is difficult to argue for life and against suicide. If we are our own "higher power," we can do with our lives what we want, or so we're told.

But if God is the Lord of all that is, he retains ownership over our lives and their days. He is the only one who can determine when our service is done, our intended purpose fulfilled. It is the clear and consistent teaching of Scripture that our lives belong to their Maker and that we are not to end them for our own purposes.

SUICIDE AND THE CATHOLIC CHURCH

Does this fact mean that suicide costs Christians their salvation?

Many of the theological questions people ask in this regard relate in some way to the Catholic Church's teachings on the subject. The Catholic Catechism contains several statements regarding suicide and mortal sin (all italics are in the original).

Suicide

The Catholic Church is clear that suicide is always a sin because our lives, ultimately, belong to God rather than to us:

#2280 Everyone is responsible for his life before God who has given it to him. It is God who remains the sovereign Master of life. We are obliged to accept life gratefully and preserve it for his honor and the salvation of our souls. We are stewards, not owners, of the life God has entrusted to us. It is not ours to dispose of (see #2281–2283).

Mortal sin

The Catholic Church, however, separates sins into two categories: "mortal" and "venial." Mortal sins separate us from God's grace; venial sins, while serious, do not (see #1037, #1470, #1859–1861, and #2268).

Theological principles

The following principles of Catholic theology seem clear:

- We cannot be sure of the spiritual state of the person who commits suicide. This person may be suffering from "grave psychological disturbances" which "can diminish the responsibility of the one committing suicide" (#2282). Mortal sin requires "full knowledge and complete consent" (#1859) and can be diminished by unintentional ignorance (#1860).

- Thus, the Church "should not despair of the eternal salvation of persons who have taken their own lives" (#2283).

- However, if the person was fully aware of his or her actions, without suffering "grave psychological disturbances," this person committed murder, an act that is "gravely sinful" (#2268).

- A person who commits a mortal sin and demonstrates "persistence in it until the end" goes to hell (#1037).

Since a person who commits self-murder (suicide) cannot then repent of this sin, it is logical to conclude that this person cannot be saved from hell. However, the Catechism nowhere makes this conclusion explicit.

IS SUICIDE THE UNPARDONABLE SIN?

Most Protestants do not believe that it is possible for a Christian to lose his or her salvation, even if that person commits suicide. And those who do typically tie that loss of salvation to a recantation of Christ rather than to a sinful act like suicide.

In this section, we'll summarize biblical principles on the subject of "eternal security." Then we'll apply them to the issue of suicide.

Know what you can know

The Bible assures us, "I write these things to you who believe in the name of the Son of God so that you may know that you have eternal life" (1 John 5:13). A literal translation would be, "We can actually and with full assurance know intellectually and personally that we have eternal life." This phrase does not mean that we gradually grow into assurance, but that we can possess here and now a present certainty of the life we have already received in Jesus.

But first we must "believe in the name of the Son of God." "Believe" means more than intellectual assent—it is the biblical word for personal trust and commitment. We can assent to the fact that an airplane will fly me from Dallas to Atlanta, but I must get on board before it can. No surgeon can operate on the basis of intellectual assent—we must submit to the procedure.

If you have made Christ your Savior, you can claim the biblical fact that you "have eternal life," present tense, right now. You are already immortal. Jesus promised that "whoever lives by believing in me will never die" (John 11:26). We simply step from time into eternity, from this life to the next.

Nowhere does the Bible say how it feels to become the child of God because our feelings can depend on the pizza we had for supper or the weather outside the window. No circumstances or events can guarantee our salvation.

It takes as much faith to believe we are Christians today as it did to become believers. We still have not seen God or proven our salvation in a test tube. And even if we had, we could question the reality or veracity of what we saw or thought.

Either the Bible is true, or it is false. Either God keeps his word, or he does not. He promises that if you "believe in the name of the Son of God," you "have eternal life" this moment. You cannot lose your salvation, for you are already the immortal child of God. This is the fact of God's word.

What about "falling from grace"?

Those who believe that it is possible to trust in Christ and then lose our salvation are quick to quote Hebrews 6:4–6. These interpreters assume that the text speaks of people who have experienced a genuine conversion, then "fall away" (v. 6). They typically believe that such a person needs another salvation experience.

But others disagree.

Some believe that the writer is stating a hypothetical case meant to emphasize why we cannot lose our salvation: if genuine Christians "have fallen away," then "it is impossible" for them "to be brought back to repentance" (vv. 4, 6). Note that if the text deals with a Christian who actually falls from faith, it teaches that the person has no chance to be saved again. The only reason that would be the case is if God decided to make such apostasy an unpardonable sin—more on this notion in a moment. It would be strange, to say the least, for the God who desires that none should perish to then deny eternal life to someone who genuinely repents simply because they had recanted that faith previously (2 Petet 3:9).

Others believe that the writer is speaking not of a Christian but of someone who considers the faith, perhaps even joins a church, but then rejects Christ. If such a person persists in unbelief, he cannot then be saved. If a person claims that he once trusted Christ but does so no more, they would conclude that he was most likely never a genuine Christian.

The Bible seems clearly to teach that a Christian is forever the child of God:

- "For God so loved the world that he gave his one and only Son, that whoever believes in him shall not perish but have eternal life" (John 3:16).

- "If anyone is in Christ, the new creation has come: The old has gone, the new is here!" (2 Corinthians 5:17).

- "My sheep listen to my voice; I know them, and they follow me. I give them eternal life, and they shall never perish; no one will snatch them out of my hand. My Father, who has given them to me, is greater than all; no one can snatch them out of my Father's hand" (John 10:27–29).

- "Everyone who lives and believes in me shall never die" (John 11:26 ESV).

What about the "unpardonable sin"?

Jesus has just healed a demon-possessed man. The crowds think he might be the Messiah, but the Pharisees say that he drives out demons by the devil himself. So, Jesus responds, "Blasphemy against the Spirit will not be forgiven" (Matthew 12:31). He repeats his warning: "Anyone who speaks a word against the Son of Man will be forgiven, but anyone who speaks against the Holy Spirit will not be forgiven, either in this age or in the age to come" (v. 32).

Peter could deny Jesus, Thomas could doubt him, and Paul could persecute his followers, yet they could be forgiven. But "blasphemy against the Spirit" cannot be forgiven, now or at any point in the future. This is the "unpardonable sin."

So, what is this sin? Let's set out what we know.

We know that Christians cannot commit this sin. The Bible is clear in 1 John 1:9: "If we confess our sins, he is faithful and just and will forgive us our sins and purify us from all unrighteousness." "All" means all. No sin is unpardonable for a Christian.

We know that this sin relates to the work of the Holy Spirit in regard to unbelievers. Jesus is warning the Pharisees, those who rejected him, that they are in danger of this sin. So, what does the Spirit do with non-Christians?

- He convicts them of their sin and need for salvation: "When [the Spirit] comes, he will prove the world to be in the wrong about sin and righteousness and judgment" (John 16:8).

- He tells them about Christ their Savior: "When the Advocate comes, whom I will send to you from the Father—the Spirit of truth who goes out from the Father—he will testify about me" (John 15:26).

- He explains salvation: "The person without the Spirit does not accept the things that come from the Spirit of God, but considers them foolishness, and cannot understand them because they are discerned only through the Spirit" (1 Corinthians 2:14).

- When they confess their sins and turn to Christ, the Spirit makes them God's children: "If anyone does not have the Spirit of Christ, they do not belong to Christ. . . . And if the Spirit of him who raised Jesus from the dead is living in you, he who raised Christ from the dead will also give life to your mortal bodies because of his Spirit who lives in you" (Romans 8:9, 11).

In short, the Holy Spirit leads lost people to salvation.

So, we know that it is the "unpardonable sin" to refuse the Spirit's work in leading you to salvation. To be convicted of your sin and need for a savior but refuse to admit it. To be presented the gospel but reject it.

Why is this sin unpardonable?

Because accepting salvation through Christ is the only means by which our sins can be pardoned.

It is "unpardonable" to reject the only surgery that can save your life or the only chemotherapy that can cure your cancer. Not because the doctor doesn't want to heal you, but because he cannot. You won't let him. You have rejected the only means of health and salvation.

The unpardonable sin is rejecting the Holy Spirit's offer of salvation and dying in such a state of rejection.

Then you have refused the only pardon God is able to give you.

Don't do that. Be sure you have made Christ your Lord, today.

To conclude this part of our conversation: no verse of Scripture connects suicide with our eternal destiny.

If this act could cause us to lose our salvation, we believe the Bible would make that fact clear. To the contrary, we can neither earn nor lose our salvation by human actions: "It is by grace you have been saved, through faith—and this is not from yourselves, it is the gift of God—not by works, so that no one can boast" (Ephesians 2:8–9).

Suicide is a tragedy for all involved, including our Father in heaven. But the Bible nowhere teaches that it costs Christians their salvation.

SUICIDE AND PHYSICIAN-ASSISTED DEATH

Physician-assisted death (PAD) is legal in ten US states and the District of Columbia. Said differently, PAD is available to one in five Americans today.

We can expect the push for PAD to increase in the future. A Gallup poll found that nearly seven in ten Americans (72 percent) say "doctors should be allowed by law to end the patient's life by some painless means if the patient and his or her family request it." This is an issue that will only increase in urgency across the coming years, but it often only discussed in general terms. Let's take a closer look at why it is important and how God would have us respond.

Euthanasia terms and concepts

"Euthanasia" is derived from the Greek words *eu* (well) and *thanatos* (death). The term usually means "a good death" or "mercy killing" and is understood to be the provision of an easy, painless death to one who suffers from an incurable or extremely painful affliction. The phrase "death with dignity" has become a popular moniker to use in place of the more technical terms.

Types of euthanasia

A distinction is usually made between "active" and "passive" euthanasia:

- Active euthanasia occurs when someone acts to produce death. This is often called "assisted suicide," as in the actions of doctors who provide medical intervention leading directly to death (such as the use of fatal injections).

- "Passive" euthanasia occurs when the patient is treated (or not treated) in a way that is intended to lead to death, but actions are not taken to cause death directly (withholding sustenance, for example).

A third category has become common in recent years. "Letting die" refers to medical actions taken to enhance the patient's well-being during the dying process. Unlike passive euthanasia, the doctor does not intend the patient to die as a result of this decision. Rather, the doctor withholds medical treatments that intensify suffering or merely postpone the moment of death for a short time. For instance, it is not considered passive euthanasia to discontinue chemotherapy in cases of advanced cancer, especially if the drugs increase the suffering of the patient. Nor is it active or passive euthanasia to elevate levels of morphine or similar medications to alleviate suffering, even if the patient may die more quickly as a result. In such cases, the physician does not intend this decision to cause death, even though death may result from his or her action.

Relevant terms

The decision to enact euthanasia is termed "non-voluntary" when patients cannot express their wishes. It would be considered "involuntary" by any who believe that it goes against the patient's wishes as he or she would have expressed them. A patient's euthanized death would be "voluntary" if he or she gave "informed consent" while motivated by his or her best interests (unlike a person suffering from mental or emotional illness who wishes to die).

A patient who executes a "durable power of attorney" assigns responsibility for medical decisions to another person, usually the spouse. In the absence of such an action, the court often assigns responsibility to the spouse, a decision known as "substituted judgment."

Using life support and/or similar technology to maintain a patient's life is termed "heroic" or "extraordinary measures." Some patients wish only "ordinary means" that offer a reasonable hope of benefit and are not excessively burdensome. A third means of support could be called "basic," providing only nutrition and water.

Doctors are required to help their patients ("beneficence") and to refrain from harming them ("non-maleficence"). They can ethically provide medical assistance to alleviate any suffering, even if such help shortens their patients' lives. This "double effect principle" assures that doctors do not act immorally if they intend only the good effect, do not use bad as a means to good, and create good at least equal to the bad. For example, as stated earlier, doctors can prescribe morphine to alleviate the suffering of a terminally ill patient, even if a side effect of morphine in that patient will shorten the person's life. They cannot, however, provide so much as to knowingly cause an overdose that will result in death.

Definitions of "death"

Doctors usually consider "death" to occur when circulation or respiration ceases irreversibly, or when the whole brain does the same. "Brain death" is a special category. The "upper brain" supports consciousness, while the brain stem controls body functions such as breathing and heart rate. If the upper brain has died, the patient is considered to be in a "persistent vegetative state" (PVS). There are estimated to be 10,000 to 25,000 PVS patients in the United States. If the brain stem has also died, the patient is considered to have suffered "brain death." Because nerve cells do not regenerate, both upper-brain and total brain death are completely irreversible.

Biblical options

At the outset, let's make it clear that active euthanasia or "assisted suicide" is unbiblical. This practice is the overt, intentional taking of life and is prohibited by the Sixth Commandment. For the remainder of this section, we will consider euthanasia only as the subject relates to passive or "letting die" options.

Defining the alternatives

Many ethicists believe that in cases of total brain death or upper-brain death, "heroic" measures are unnecessary. Many believe that ordinary treatment is not obligatory and "letting die" is moral. Some, however, believe that it is wrong to withdraw food and hydration, allowing the body to starve.

This approach views the life as "holistic," meaning that a functioning body is still united to the "soul," the "image of God." Such a person is still a member of the human race and deserves at least basic care (food and water), if not ordinary care (routine medical support).

Other Christians believe that brain-dead or PVS patients are simply bodies, that their souls or spiritual selves have gone on to eternity. Withdrawing food and water from such patients is then considered to be morally acceptable.

In this view, without a functioning brain, the body no longer sustains a soul or retains the image of God. Medical personnel should always care for those who possess the potential for conscious life. But when a PVS exists, there is no possibility of brain regeneration and the "soul" has left the body.

Still others support "vitalism," the belief that physical function by itself is sacred. In this view, even if the "soul" has departed a body that is brain-dead or in a PVS, the body deserves medical treatment to the very end of physical life. Some "vitalists" support ordinary care or basic care for such a body, while others argue for heroic means to preserve physical function as long as possible.

Which view is the most biblical?

Created in the image of God

One way to answer our question involves the scriptural description of humanity as created "in God's image." Genesis says that "God created man in his own image, in the image of God he created him; male and female he created them" (Genesis 1:27). What does it mean to be made in God's "image"?

Most theologians focus on humanity's uniqueness. What is it that separates us from other forms of life? Such characteristics make us uniquely "the image of God." Four biblical statements address the question:

- We are created in God's image to "have dominion over" his creation (Genesis 1:28).

- The Lord warns us, "Whoever sheds the blood of man, by man shall his blood be shed, for God made man in his own image" (Genesis 9:6).

- Paul states that a man is "the image and glory of God" (1 Corinthians 11:7).

- James states that people are "made in the likeness of God" (James 3:9).

From these specific biblical references to the "image" or "likeness" of God, we can suggest that a person retains this "image" when he or she is able to relate to the rest of God's creation as his representative on earth. We are to "rule" or govern creation, represent God to others, and value each other. In this sense, we are "in" his image so long as we manifest his image on earth. By this reasoning, we lose the "image of God," that which makes us uniquely human and valuable, when we lose the ability or potential to relate to ourselves, our environment, other humans, and God. A baby in the womb and a comatose patient are each a person in that they retain the potential for such interaction. But a PVS individual is not.

Dualistic and holistic views

How does this distinction relate to the body?

Some believe that the "soul" can depart the body before its physical death. This is typically considered the "dualistic" view, separating the physical and the spiritual. Jesus cried from the cross, "Father, into your hands I commit my spirit!" (Luke 23:46). Stephen prayed before his physical death, "Lord Jesus, receive my spirit" (Acts 7:59). Some interpreters use these statements to separate the soul or "image of God" from the body. In the belief that a PVS patient does not and cannot exhibit the image of God, it is then concluded that the person's "soul" has left the body. Any physical support for the body, even food and water, is thus unnecessary.

Others adopt a holistic understanding of the biblical view of humans. While Greek philosophy separated body, soul, and spirit, Hebrew theology did not. It is not that we *have* a body, soul, and spirit that can be identified as separate entities. Rather, we *are* body, soul, and spirit. These words are different dimensions of the one person (cf. 1 Thessalonians 5:23). In the holistic view, we retain the "image of God" so long as our bodies retain some dimension of physical life. In this approach, so long as a person is alive physically, that person is the "image of God." Food and water would be essential, appropriate provision for any person. And so, the decision to withdraw food and water would be wrong.

Permission to die?

What if a patient previously directed that such withdrawal occur? Then the law would require that his or her wishes be honored. But should it? Should we be permitted to mandate that heroic or even ordinary measures *not* be taken to maintain our lives?

The dualistic view believes that a patient loses the "image of God" in certain medical conditions and would support that person's previously stated right to refuse medical life support. The holistic view, taken to its logical conclusion, would seem to require at least food and water to be provided in the desire to preserve and honor the "image of God." It could be argued that even heroic measures are required and that a person should not be allowed to refuse them. Just as we require passengers in cars and airplanes to wear seat belts, so we should require patients to receive all medical support for as long as their bodies survive.

My position

I believe that the holistic view reflects God's understanding of humanity. But I also believe a distinction between heroic, ordinary, and basic life support is warranted. In my view, it is permissible to cease heroic or even ordinary life support for a person who possesses no actual or potential capacity for relational life on any level, as that person cannot demonstrate the "image of God." But I also believe that, so long as the body is alive, the "person" is alive. And persons deserve at least basic support (food and water) for as long as they live.

However, we and/or our doctors can choose to "let die," to take medical steps that do not prolong our lives. When these medical actions enhance the present quality of life, even if they shorten the life span of terminally ill patients, they are especially warranted.

Medical care and the power of God

In dealing with family members facing end-of-life decisions, here are the questions I think we should ask:

- Do they intend to hasten or even cause death? I do not believe such a decision is defensible.

- On the other hand, do they wish simply to allow nature to take over, "letting die" if this is the natural result of the patient's condition? In this situation, medical support is not prolonging life—it is prolonging death.

Maintaining or ending medical care does not necessarily affect the intervention of God. The Lord Jesus raised Lazarus from the grave after he had been dead four days (John 11:38–44). God does not require medical life support to heal.

If all medical options have been exhausted and there is no plausible reason to believe the patient will ever improve, a family who ends heroic or ordinary life support is not removing the possibility of divine intervention. Rather, they are placing their loved one in God's hands, allowing him to heal physically or eternally.

HELP FOR THOSE CONSIDERING SUICIDE

People consider suicide when the pain they feel exceeds their ability to cope with it. They want to end their suffering and think that ending their lives will bring relief.

If you or someone you know is having thoughts of suicide, please get help immediately.

Ask your pastor to recommend a Christian counselor in your area.

You can call the 988 Suicide & Crisis Lifeline by dialing 988 or visit 988lifeline.org.

Take every threat of suicide seriously.

In the meanwhile, it is important to know that it is possible to get through this.

Feeling suicidal does not require that we act on our feelings. The best thing to do immediately is to create some space. If we decide not to act on our feelings for even a few minutes or a day, we can find the strength to seek help. By seeking help, we can deal with the pain and find the hope we need.

Warning signs

The Centers for Disease Control lists these twelve "suicide warning signs":

- Feeling like a burden
- Being isolated
- Increased anxiety
- Feeling trapped or in unbearable pain
- Increased substance use
- Looking for a way to access lethal means
- Increased anger or rage
- Extreme mood swings
- Expressing hopelessness
- Sleeping too little or too much
- Talking or posting about wanting to die
- Making plans for suicide

This is an issue parents need to discuss with their children. Read Janet Denison's article, "The Kate Spade Conversation" at foundationswithjanet.org. She discusses the major rise in depression among teenagers and links to an important article by the Society to Prevent Teenage Suicide. And she notes that "too often, Christians feel that depression should simply be handled 'spiritually' instead of 'medically.' Depression is an illness, and an illness needs both types of help. While medicine alone is unlikely to be the cure, sometimes it's needed to get a person to the place where they're able to take the additional steps necessary to see real improvement. If you have reason to believe you and/or your child are clinically depressed, you and your child need the help of a physician, as well as the Great Physician."

Protective factors

The following indicators help buffer people from the risks associated with suicide:

- Effective clinical care for mental, physical, and substance abuse disorders

- Easy access to clinical interventions and support for those seeking help

- Family and community support

- Support from ongoing medical and mental health care relationships

- Skills in problem-solving, conflict resolution, and nonviolent ways of handling disputes

- Cultural and religious beliefs that discourage suicide and encourage self-preservation instincts

Help those you care about to experience these positive influences and you'll do much to prevent the tragedy of suicide.

THREE BIBLICAL PROMISES

In the appendix of his classic book, *The Problem of Pain*, C. S. Lewis includes this note from physician R. Havard: "Mental pain is less dramatic than physical pain, but it is more common and also harder to bear. The frequent attempt to conceal mental pain increases the burden: it is easier to say 'My tooth is aching' than to say 'My heart is broken.'"

Let's close by claiming three promises God makes to every suffering person today.

One: You and every person you know is someone of inestimable worth.

Depression and life crises can cause us to feel that our lives are not worth living. The opposite is true. Every person on earth is someone for whom Jesus died (Romans 5:8).

In 1941, C. S. Lewis preached his famous "Weight of Glory" sermon in St. Mary's Chapel at Oxford University. In it, he stated, "There are no *ordinary* people. You have never talked to a mere mortal. Nations, cultures, arts, civilizations—these are mortal, and their life is to ours as the life of a gnat" (his emphasis).

Lewis adds: "Next to the Blessed Sacrament itself, your neighbor is the holiest object presented to your senses."

And if you are the one struggling with suicidal thoughts or the depression that can so easily lead to that end, know that there is no shame in those thoughts or feelings and that your life does matter. The Lord of all creation chose to give you life for a reason. And while it can be easy to lose sight of that fact from time to time, it doesn't change the reality that your life matters to God.

Please make sure it matters to you as well.

Two: God loves you and wants to help.

When Elijah despaired of his life and prayed, "It is enough; now, O Lord, take away my life" (1 Kings 19:4 ESV), God provided the physical, spiritual, and emotional sustenance he needed to go on. When Jeremiah said, "Cursed be the day I was born!" (Jeremiah 20:14), God sustained his prophet.

Scripture promises: "The Lord is close to the brokenhearted and saves those who are crushed in spirit" (Psalm 34:18). Paul, who faced almost indescribable challenges (2 Corinthians 11:23–28), could proclaim, "I consider that our present sufferings are not worth comparing with the glory that will be revealed in us" (Romans 8:18).

Jesus knows your pain. He has faced everything we face (Hebrews 4:15). He cried from the cross, "My God, my God, why have you forsaken me?" (Matthew 27:46). Now he is ready to help you.

However, let me repeat that one of the most important ways the Great Physician heals is through human physicians. That's why you need to reach out to professional counselors as soon as possible. God will use them as he ministers his grace to you.

Three: You can "dwell on the heights" with God.

Paul testified that he could "take captive every thought to make it obedient to Christ" (2 Corinthians 10:5).

He could do this because he lived in the power of the Holy Spirit (Ephesians 5:18).

God wants to be "the sure foundation for your times, a rich store of salvation and wisdom and knowledge" (Isaiah 33:6). The person who walks with him "will dwell on the heights" (v. 16).

You can "dwell on the heights" with your Father. This is the promise, and the invitation, of God.

Will you accept it today?

A DISCUSSION GUIDE ON SUICIDE

The following discussion guide may be used in a small group setting or for your personal time of devotion. We hope it helps you both better understand the topic and how God might want to use you, in your specific context, to be "salt and light" on this issue.

NOTE: If you or someone you know is having thoughts of suicide, please get help immediately. Ask your pastor to recommend a Christian counselor in your area. Call or text the 988 Suicide & Crisis Lifeline at 988 or visit 988lifeline.org. Take every threat of suicide seriously.

1. When a famous person dies by suicide, how does it make you feel?

2. Have you ever experienced someone close to you dying by suicide? How did you react? What do you wish you would have known or done before their decision?

3. Does our culture accept suicide? What evidence proves your stance?

4. What have you learned in church about suicide?

5. Do you believe that a Christian who commits suicide will enter heaven? What biblical proof can you cite?

6. How does the question of "the unpardonable sin" relate to whether a Christian can lose his or her salvation? Put another way, can a Christian "fall from grace"?

7. Does our culture accept physician-assisted suicide? What evidence proves your stance?

8. Have you ever given thought to what "extreme measures" you would allow to yourself if placed in a medically precarious position? Or have you had a personal experience with family or friends facing such decisions? How did they decide their chosen path?

9. If you had an aggressive disease and had been given only months to live, would you seek quantity of life or quality of life? Why?

10. What does it mean to be created in God's image? How does this fact relate to physician-assisted suicide?

11. How do the dualistic and holistic views of the body differ?

12. How can you help others dealing with anxiety, depression, and/or thoughts of suicide?

13. What are three promises of God every Christian can claim when it comes to the problem of suicide?

6

THE MORAL ISSUE OF OUR TIME

What does the Bible say about abortion?

When the Supreme Court overturned *Roe v. Wade*, thereby sending the issue of abortion back to the states for the first time since 1973, many understandably proclaimed it a victory for the sanctity of life. And, in many ways, it was. The number of abortions has dropped dramatically in states like Texas, Tennessee, Georgia, and a host of others that have passed laws intended to restrict access to it.

Yet many other states have expanded access to abortion, in some cases well beyond what was legal when *Roe v. Wade* was still the law of the land. Those new laws, combined with increased access to pharmaceutical abortifacients even in states where abortion is otherwise restricted, have meant that 2023 actually saw an increase in the total number of unborn lives lost to abortion.

Clearly, overturning *Roe* was not enough, and it was never going to be. So where do we go from here?

Given that nearly 70 percent of Americans support at least some access to abortion during the first trimester—though that support wanes quickly in the second trimester and beyond—it's unlikely that the issue is going away anytime soon. Moreover, while politicians on both sides have pressed for passing federal legislation on the subject as well, neither side appears close to having the necessary support to do so without opening a Pandora's box of related issues. As such, it is likely that abortion law will remain with the states for the foreseeable future.

And, ultimately, that's probably for the best.

It may not feel that way as we watch state after state make it permissible to kill the unborn, often even when the child could survive outside the womb. But the truth is, we should want this issue to remain with the states because that's the level of government where we can have the greater impact. After all, in a democracy your vote is worth more in elections where fewer votes are cast.

So how can we do that?

It starts by shifting our focus from politics to people. But in order to do that well, we need to have a strong understanding of not only what we believe but why we believe it.

Abortion is *the* moral issue of our time.

Most conservative Christians believe that life begins at conception and abortion is therefore wrong. But are we sure? Is this a biblical fact?

If the answer is clear, why have so many denominational leaders taken pro-choice positions?

Is there a biblical, cohesive, practical position on this difficult subject?

To answer those questions, let's start by defining some terms to ensure we're all on the same page when it comes to what's actually being debated.

PRO-LIFE VS. PRO-CHOICE

An "abortion" occurs when a "conceptus" is caused to die. To clarify vocabulary, "conceptus" is a general term for preborn life growing in the mother's womb.

More specifically, doctors often speak of the union of a sperm and an ovum as a "zygote." A growing zygote is an "embryo." When the embryo reaches around seven weeks of age, it is called a "fetus." However, "fetus" is usually used in the abortion debate to describe all preborn life.

- A "miscarriage" is a spontaneous, natural abortion.

- An "indirect abortion" occurs when actions taken to cure the mother's illness cause the unintended death of the fetus.

- A "direct abortion" occurs when action is taken to cause the intended death of the fetus.

Why do so many people in America believe that a mother should have the right to choose direct abortion?

In 1973, the Supreme Court issued *Roe v. Wade*, its landmark abortion ruling. In essence, the Court overturned state laws limiting a woman's right to abortion. Its decision was largely based on the argument that the Constitution nowhere defines a fetus as a person or protects the rights of the unborn.

Rather, the Court determined that an unborn baby possesses only "potential life" and is not yet a "human being" or "person." It argued that every constitutional reference to "person" relates to those already born. The Fourteenth Amendment guarantees protections and rights to individuals, but the Court ruled that the amendment does not include the unborn.

The Court further determined that a woman's "right to privacy" extends to her ability to make her own choices regarding her health and body. Just as she has the right to choose to become pregnant, she has the right to end that pregnancy.

The Court suggested several specific reasons why she might choose abortion:

- "specific and direct harm" may come to her

- "maternity, or additional offspring, may force upon the woman a distressful life and future"

- "psychological harm may be imminent"

- "mental and physical health may be taxed by child care"

- problems may occur associated with bearing unwanted children

- and "the additional difficulties and continuing stigma of unwed motherhood" should be considered.

Since 1973, four positions have been taken in the abortion debate:

- There should be no right to an abortion, even to save the life of the mother. This has been the Catholic Church's usual position.

- Therapeutic abortions can be performed to save the mother's life.

- Extreme case abortions can be permitted in cases of rape, incest, or severe deformation of the fetus. Most pro-life advocates would accept therapeutic and extreme case abortions.

- Abortion should be available to any woman who chooses it. This is the typical "pro-choice" position.

MORAL ARGUMENTS FOR ABORTION

"Pro-choice" advocates make five basic claims:

1. No one can say when a fetus becomes a person, so the mother is the most appropriate person to make decisions regarding it.

2. Abortion must be protected so a woman who is the victim of rape or incest does not have to bear a child resulting from such an attack.

3. No unwanted child should be brought into the world.

4. The state has no right to legislate personal morality.

5. A woman must be permitted to make pregnancy decisions in light of her life circumstances.

Many theologians, pastors, and denominational leaders consider these claims to be both biblical and moral.

First, "pro-choice" proponents argue that a fetus is not legally a "person."

They agree with the Supreme Court's finding that the Constitution nowhere grants legal standing to a preborn life. Only 40 to 50 percent of fetuses survive to become persons in the full sense. A fetus belongs to the mother until it attains personhood and is morally subject to any action she wishes to take with it.

Second, abortion must be protected as an alternative for women who are the victims of rape or incest.

While this number is admittedly small in this country (approximately one percent of all abortions), it is growing in many countries around the world. As many as one in three women may become the victim of such an attack. They argue that these women must be spared the further trauma of pregnancy and childbirth.

Third, no unwanted children should be brought into the world.

If a woman does not wish to bear a child, she clearly will not be an appropriate or effective mother if the child is born. Given the population explosion occurring in many countries of the world, abortion is a necessary option for women who do not want children. The woman is more closely involved with the fetus than any other individual and is the best person to determine whether or not this child is wanted and will receive proper care.

Fourth, the state has no right to legislate our personal moral decisions.

The government has no authority to restrict homosexuality, consensual sex, cigarette consumption, or other individual decisions that many people consider to be wrong. Since there is no constitutional standard for when life begins, decisions made regarding a fetus are likewise a matter for individual morality.

The state should impose legislation on moral questions only when this legislation expresses the clear moral consensus of the community and when it prevents conduct which obviously threatens the public welfare. Nearly everyone condemns murder, for instance, and believes that it threatens us all. But Americans are divided on the morality of abortion. It is hard to see how aborting a fetus threatens the rest of the community.

And so abortion should not be subject to governmental control. It is better to allow a mother to make this decision than to legislate it through governmental action. Many who personally consider abortion to be wrong are persuaded by this argument and thus support the "pro-choice" position.

Fifth, the rights and concerns of the mother must take precedence over those of the fetus.

Even if we grant fetuses limited rights, they must not supersede the rights of mothers, as the latter are clearly persons under the Constitution. If we allow abortion to protect her physical life, we should do so to protect her emotional health or quality of life as well.

This was one of the Court's most significant arguments, as it sought to protect the mother's mental and physical health. Many "pro-choice" advocates are especially persuaded by this argument and view the abortion debate within the context of a woman's right to control her own life.

MORAL ARGUMENTS AGAINST ABORTION

"Pro-life" advocates counter each of these claims with their own ethical arguments.

First, they assert that a fetus is a human life and should be granted the full protection of the law.

The fetus carries its parents' genetic code and is a distinct person. It does not yet possess self-consciousness, reasoning ability, or moral awareness (the usual descriptions of a "person"), but neither do newborns or young children. As this is the central issue of the debate, we'll say more about it in a moment.

Second, most "pro-life" advocates are willing to permit abortion in cases of rape or incest or to protect the life of the mother.

Since such cases typically account for only one to four percent of abortions performed, limiting abortion to these conditions would prevent the vast majority of abortions occurring in America.

Third, "pro-life" advocates agree that all children should be wanted, so they argue strongly for adoption as an alternative to abortion.

They also assert that an unwanted child would rather live than die. By "pro-choice" logic, it would be possible to argue for infanticide and all forms of euthanasia as well as abortion.

Fourth, "pro-life" supporters do not see abortion legislation as an intrusion into areas of private morality.

Protecting the rights of the individual is the state's first responsibility. No moral state can overlook murder, whatever the personal opinions of those who commit it. The state is especially obligated to protect the rights of those who cannot defend themselves.

But what of the claim that legislation must always reflect the clear will of the majority and protect the public welfare?

If more of the public understood the physical and ethical issues involved in abortion, the large majority would consider abortion to be a threat to public welfare. Abortion threatens the entire community in three ways:

1. Abortion ends the lives of millions, on a level exceeding all wars and disasters combined.

2. Abortion encourages sexual promiscuity.

3. Abortion permits women to make a choice that will plague many of them with guilt for years to come.

And so abortion meets the standard for legislative relevance and must be addressed and limited or abolished by the state.

Fifth, "pro-life" advocates want to encourage the health of both the mother and the child and do not believe that we must choose between the two.

As the rights of a mother are no more important than those of her newborn infant, so they are no more important than those of her preborn child. The stress, guilt, and long-term mental anguish reported by many who abort their children must be considered. The legal right to abortion subjects a woman to pressure from her husband or sexual partner to end her pregnancy.

Killing the fetus for the sake of the mother's health is like remedying paranoia by killing all the imagined persecutors. For these reasons, "pro-life" advocates argue that a moral state must limit or prevent abortion.

(For more on the ethical arguments for and against abortion see Milton A. Gonsalves' *Right & Reason: Ethics in Theory and Practice*, 9th ed.)

WHEN DOES LIFE BEGIN?

This is obviously the crucial question in the abortion debate.

If life does not begin until the fetus is viable or the child is born, one can argue that the "right to life" does not extend to the preborn and abortion should be considered both legal and moral.

But if life begins at conception, there can be no moral justification for abortion, since this action kills an innocent person.

There are essentially three answers to our question:

- **"Functionalism"** states that the fetus is a "person" when it can act personally as a moral, intellectual, and spiritual agent. (Note that by this definition, some question whether a newborn infant would be considered a "person.")

- **"Actualism"** is the position that a fetus is a person if it possesses the potential for developing self-conscious, personal life. This definition would permit abortion when the fetus clearly does not possess the capacity for functional life.

- **"Essentialism"** argues that the fetus is a person from conception, whatever its health or potential. It is an individual in the earliest stages of development and deserves all the protections afforded to other persons by our society.

Our Declaration of Independence begins, "We hold these truths to be self-evident: that all men are created equal; that they are endowed by their creator with certain inalienable rights; that among these are life, liberty, and the pursuit of happiness." If an unborn child is considered a person, it possesses the "inalienable" right to life as well.

So, can we determine when life begins?

Our answer depends on the definition of *life*.

A "pro-choice" advocate recognizes that the fetus is alive in the sense that it is a biological entity. But so is every other part of a woman's body. Some consider the fetus to be a "growth" and liken it to a tumor or other unwanted tissue. Biology alone is not enough to settle the issue.

What about capacity?

Many ethicists define a "person" as someone able to respond to stimuli, interact with others, and make individual decisions. A fetus meets the first two standards from almost the moment of its conception, and clearly cannot fulfill the third only because it is enclosed in its mother's body. Is a newborn baby inherently able to fulfill these three conditions any better than a child still in the womb?

What about individuality?

If we view a fetus as a "growth" within the mother's body, it would be easier to sanction her choice to remove that growth if she wishes. But a fetus is distinct from its mother from the moment of its conception.

- It is alive: it reacts to stimuli and can produce its own cells and develop them into a specific pattern of maturity.

- It is human, completely distinguishable from all other living organisms, possessing all forty-six human chromosomes, able to develop only into a human being.

- And it is complete: nothing new will be added except the growth and development of what exists from the moment of conception.

It is a scientific fact that every abortion performed in the United States is performed on a being so fully formed that its heart is beating and its brain activity can be measured on an EEG machine. At twelve weeks, the unborn baby is only about two inches long, yet every organ of the human body is clearly in place.

Theologian Karl Barth described the fetus well:

> The embryo has its own autonomy, its own brain, its own nervous system, its own blood circulation. If its life is affected by that of the mother, it also affects hers. It can have its own illnesses in which the mother has no part. Conversely, it may be quite healthy even though the mother is seriously ill. It may die while the mother continues to live. It may also continue to live after its mother's death, and be eventually saved by a timely operation on her dead body. In short, it is a human being in its own right.

And note that you did not come from a fetus—you were a fetus. A "fetus" is simply a human life in the womb. It becomes a "baby" outside the womb. But it is the same physical entity in either place.

For these reasons, "pro-life" advocates believe that the US Supreme Court was wrong in deciding that a fetus is not a person entitled to the full protections of the law and that any state where abortion continues to be protected is wrong as well.

Apart from spiritual or moral concerns, it is a simple fact of biology that the fetus possesses every attribute of human life we find in a newborn infant, with the exception of independent physical viability. Left unharmed, it will soon develop this capacity as well. If a life must be independently viable to be viewed as a person, a young child might well fail this standard, as would those of any age facing severe physical challenges.

WHAT DOES THE BIBLE SAY ABOUT ABORTION?

These statements are based on moral claims and legal arguments. They are intended to persuade society regardless of a person's religious persuasion. But many in our culture also want to know what the Bible says on this crucial subject.

Does the Bible talk about abortion?

The word *abortion* appears nowhere in the Bible.

No one in the Bible is ever described as having an abortion, encouraging one, or even dealing with one.

The Bible says nothing which specifically addresses our subject.

And so many have concluded that the issue is not a biblical concern but a private matter. They say that we should be silent where the Bible is silent.

"Pro-life" advocates counter that by this logic we should be silent regarding the "Trinity" since the word never appears in Scripture. Or "marijuana" and "cocaine" since they are not in a biblical concordance. However, these issues came after the biblical era, while abortion was common in the ancient world. So this argument doesn't seem relevant.

If abortion is a biblical issue, why doesn't the Bible address it specifically?

The answer is simple: the Jewish people and first Christians needed no such guidance. It was an undeniable fact of their faith and culture that abortion was wrong. How do we know?

Consider early statements on the subject.

The *Sentences of Pseudo-Phocylides* is a book of Jewish wisdom written between 50 BC and AD 50. They state that "a woman should not destroy the unborn babe in her belly, nor after its birth throw it before the dogs and vultures as a prey."

The *Sibylline Oracles* are an ancient work of Jewish theology. They include among the wicked two groups: women who "produce abortions and unlawfully cast their offspring away" and sorcerers who dispense materials which cause abortions (2:339-42).

The *Mishnah* ("instruction") was the written record of Jewish oral teachings transmitted since the time of Moses. These teachings were committed to writing around 200 B.C.

In the Mishnah tractate *Sanhedrin* we read: "We infer the death penalty for killing an embryo from the text, *He who sheds the blood of a man within a man, his blood shall be shed*; what is 'a man within a man'? An embryo" (Sanhedrin 57b, quoting Genesis 9:6).

An abortion was permitted only to save the life of the mother: "If a woman was in hard travail [life-threatening labor], the child must be cut up while it is in the womb and brought out member by member, since the life of the mother has priority over the life of the child; but if the great part of it was already born, it may not be touched, since the claim of one life cannot override the claim of another life" (Oholoth 7:6).

The Jews in the Old and New Testaments did not need to address the issue of abortion since no one considered it a moral option.

When the Christian church moved out of its Jewish context, it encountered a culture that accepted the practice of abortion. And so, after the New Testament, Christians began speaking specifically to the subject.

For instance, the *Didache* (the earliest theological treatise after the Bible) states: "You shall not procure [an] abortion, nor destroy a newborn child."

And the *Epistle of Barnabas* (early second century) adds, "Thou shalt love thy neighbor more than thy own life. Thou shalt not procure abortion, thou shalt not commit infanticide."

These books were widely read and accepted in the first centuries of the Christian church.

Important biblical passages about abortion

While the Bible does not use the word *abortion*, it contains a number of texts that relate directly to the beginning of life and the value of all persons. Let's look briefly at the most pertinent passages.

Exodus 21:22

"Pro-choice" scholars usually begin the discussion with this statement in Exodus: "When people who are fighting injure a pregnant woman so that there is a miscarriage, and yet no further harm follows, the one responsible shall be fined what the woman's husband demands, paying as much as the judges determine. If any harm follows, then you shall give life for life, eye for eye, tooth for tooth, hand for hand, foot for foot, burn for burn, wound for wound, stripe for stripe" (Exodus 21:22–25).

The ancient Jewish historian Flavius Josephus commented on this text: "He that kicks a woman with child, so that the woman miscarry, let him pay a fine in money, as the judges shall determine, as having diminished the multitude by the destruction of what was in her womb; and let money also be given to the woman's husband by him that kicked her; but if she die of the stroke, let him also be put to death, the law judging it equitable that life should go for life."

But notice the translator's note: "The law seems rather to mean, that if the infant be killed, though the mother escape, the offender must be put to death; and not only when the mother is killed, as Josephus understood it."

And note this later statement by Josephus: "The law, moreover, enjoins us to bring up all our offspring, and forbids women to cause abortion of what is begotten, or to destroy it afterward; and if any woman appears to have done so, she will be a murderer of her child, by destroying a living creature, and diminishing human kind."

If this text does indeed teach that a person causing a miscarriage is only to be fined, while one causing "harm" is to receive severe punishment, we would have an important indication that the fetus is not as valuable as its mother. Is this what the text clearly teaches?

The New Revised Standard renders the text, "so that there is a miscarriage." The New American Standard follows suit, as does the New Jerusalem Bible. But the New International Version translates the text, "she gives birth prematurely but there is no serious injury." The New Living Translation similarly states, "they hurt a pregnant woman so that her child is born prematurely. If no further harm results . . ." The English Standard Version renders the phrase, "so that her children come out, but there is no harm." Why this crucial difference in translation?

The Hebrew phrase is literally rendered, "And they come forth children of her." "Children" is the plural of *yeled*, the usual Hebrew word for child or offspring (the Hebrew language has no separate word for "fetus" or the preborn). "Come forth" translates *yatsa*, a word which does not specify whether the child is alive or dead, only that it leaves the womb. And so the Hebrew of Exodus 21:22 does not indicate whether the woman suffered a miscarriage (NRSV, NASB, NJB) or experienced a premature healthy birth (NIV, NLT, ESV). But it does refer to the fetus as a "child." And it is important to note that the text does not use *shachol*, the Hebrew word for "miscarriage" (this word is found in Exodus 23:26 and Hosea 9:14 among other occurrences).

(For further discussion of this linguistic issue see Jack W. Cottrell's "Abortion and the Mosaic Law" in *Readings in Christian Ethics*.)

Verse 23 settles the issue for me: "But if there is serious injury . . ." (NIV), implying that no serious injury occurred in verse 22. In other words, both the mother and her child survived the attack and were healthy. And so this passage does not devalue the preborn life or speak specifically to the issue of abortion.

Genesis 2:7

The Bible describes man's creation in this way: "In the day that the Lord God made the earth and the heavens, when no plant of the field was yet in the earth and no herb of the field had yet sprung up–for the Lord God had not caused it to rain upon the earth, and there was no one to till the ground; but a stream would rise from the earth, and water the whole face of the ground–then the Lord God formed man from the dust of the ground, and breathed into his nostrils the breath of life; and the man became a living being" (Genesis 2:4–7).

It seems that Adam did not become a "living being" until he could breathe. And so some believe that a fetus is not a "living being" until it can breathe outside the mother's womb. Until this time it is not yet a person.

President Bill Clinton explained his pro-choice position as based significantly on this logic. He said that his pastor, W. O. Vaught, former pastor of Immanuel Baptist Church in Little Rock, Arkansas, told him that this was the literal meaning of the text.

There are three problems with this argument.

1. Adam was an inanimate object until God breathed into him "the breath of life," but we know conclusively that a fetus is animate from the moment of conception.

2. The fetus breathes in the womb, exchanging amniotic fluid for air after birth.

3. Adam in Genesis 2:7 was a potential life even before he became a human being. By any definition, a fetus is at the very least a potential human being. We'll say more about this fact in a moment.

Psalm 139

One of David's best-loved psalms contains this affirmation:

> For it was you who formed my inward parts; you knit me together in my mother's womb. I praise you, for I am fearfully and wonderfully made. Wonderful are your works; that I know very well. My frame was not hidden from you, when I was being made in secret, intricately woven in the depths of the earth. Your eyes beheld my unformed substance. In your book were written all the days that were formed for me, when none of them as yet existed. (Psalm 139:13–16)

David clearly believed that God created him in his mother's womb and "beheld my unformed substance" before he was born. "Pro-life" theologians point to this declaration as proof that life is created by God and begins at conception.

Of course, those who do not accept the authority of Scripture will not be persuaded by this argument. And some who do believe that David's statement is poetic symbolism rather than scientific description. He is simply stating that he is God's creation, without speaking specifically to the status of a fetus.

Jeremiah 1:5

As part of God's call to the prophet Jeremiah, the Lord issued this declaration: "Before I formed you in the womb I knew you, and before you were born I consecrated you; I appointed you a prophet to the nations" (Jeremiah 1:5). God clearly formed Jeremiah in the womb and "knew" him even before that time. He "consecrated" or called him to special service even before he was born. God's plan for Jeremiah began before his conception and his birth.

It's hard for me to see how those who accept biblical authority could make a "pro-choice" response to this statement. I suppose they could claim that the verse is symbolic and spiritual, not scientific, that it is a metaphorical description of God's eternal plan for Jeremiah. But the text seems to be specifically related to Jeremiah's conception and gestation.

Luke 1:39–45

Luke's gospel records the visit of the pregnant Mary to the pregnant Elizabeth: "In those days Mary set out and went with haste to a Judean town in the hill country, where she entered the house of Zechariah and greeted Elizabeth. When Elizabeth heard Mary's greeting, the child leaped in her womb. And Elizabeth was filled with the Holy Spirit and exclaimed with a loud cry, "Blessed are you among women, and blessed is the fruit of your womb. And why has this happened to me, that the mother of my Lord comes to me? For as soon as I heard the sound of your greeting, the child in my womb leaped for joy. And blessed is she who believed that there would be a fulfillment of what was spoken to her by the Lord" (Luke 1:39–45).

When Elizabeth said that "the child in my womb leaped for joy" (v. 44), she made clear the fact that her "fetus" was a fully responding being. She used the word *brephos*, the Greek term for baby, embryo, fetus, newborn child, young child, or nursing child. It is the same word used to describe Jesus in the manger, where the shepherds "went with haste and found Mary and Joseph, and the *child* lying in the manger" (Luke 2:16).

Paul used the word in reminding Timothy "how from *childhood* you have known the sacred writings that are able to instruct you for salvation through faith in Christ Jesus" (2 Timothy 3:15). The Bible makes no linguistic distinction between the personhood of a human being, whether before or after its birth.

What are the rights of the innocent?

The Bible consistently defends the rights of those who are innocent and undeserving of punishment or death. For instance:

- "Do not kill the innocent and those in the right, for I will not acquit the guilty" (Exodus 23:7).

- "There are six things that the Lord hates, seven that are an abomination to him: haughty eyes, a lying tongue, and hands that shed innocent blood, a heart that devises wicked plans, feet that hurry to run to evil, a lying witness who testifies falsely, and one who sows discord in a family" (Proverbs 6:16–19).

- The Babylonians attacked Jerusalem "for the sins of Manasseh, for all that he had committed, and also for the innocent blood that he had shed; for he filled Jerusalem with innocent blood, and the Lord was not willing to pardon" (2 Kings 24:3–4).

It is clear that God cares for the innocent and defenseless of the world. Children, whether before their birth or after, would be among his most valued creations.

HOW HAVE CHRISTIANS VIEWED ABORTION?

How has the Church viewed the issue of abortion across its history?

Are "pro-choice" religious leaders in step with traditional Christian thinking on this subject? Or has the Church even spoken with a unified voice when addressing the question?

Early church fathers were clear in their opposition to abortion.

Athenagoras (ca. AD 150), Clement of Alexandria (ca. 150–215), Tertullian (ca. 155–225), St. Hippolytus (ca. 170–236), St. Basil the Great (ca. 330–79), St. Ambrose (ca. 339–97), St. John Chrysostom (ca. 340–407), and St. Jerome (ca. 342–420) all issued strong condemnations of this practice.

However, these theologians did not specifically say when the body receives a soul. This is the process called "animation" or "ensoulment" by early philosophers. Many in the ancient world followed the thinking of Aristotle (384–322 BC) on the issue. He believed that "ensoulment" occurred forty days after conception in males and ninety days in females, and taught that abortion prior to this time was not murder.

St. Augustine of Hippo (354–430), arguably the greatest theological mind after Paul, can be quoted on both sides of the issue. As regards whether souls are given to bodies at conception, Augustine said, "He . . . who formed them, knows whether He formed them with the soul, or gave the soul to them after they had been formed. . . . I have no certain knowledge how it came into my body; for it was not I who gave it to myself." He was critical of a theologian who was too dogmatic on this issue, claiming, "how much better it is for him to share my hesitation about the soul's origin." He did not believe that we can know when people "obtain their souls."

And yet Augustine was convinced that those who die in the womb will be resurrected with the rest of humanity and given perfect bodies in heaven. If they died, they must have lived; if they lived, they will be resurrected. Babies deformed at birth will be given perfect bodies in paradise as well (*Enchiridion* 85). It would seem that Augustine believed life to begin at conception, as the moment the fetus can die, it must have been alive.

Theologians, popes, and church councils in the centuries to follow would continue to debate this issue. St. Jerome (ca. 342–420) could speak of the "murder of an unborn child" (Letter 22:13), and yet he could state that abortion is not killing until the fetus acquires limbs and shape (Letter 121:4). Pope Innocent III (ca. 1161–1216) stated that the soul enters the body of the fetus when the woman feels the first movement of the fetus (the "quickening"). After such "ensoulment," abortion is murder; previously it is a less serious sin, as it ends only potential human life.

Thomas Aquinas (1225?–74) condemned abortion for any and all reasons. However, he agreed with Aristotle's conclusion that a male child was formed enough to be judged human at forty days, a female at eighty. Only when the fetus could be considered human could it have a soul.

On the other hand, Pope Leo XIII (1878–1903) issued a decree in 1886 that prohibited all procedures which directly kill the fetus, even to save the life of the mother. He also required excommunication for abortions at any stage of pregnancy.

To summarize, Christian leaders across church history have been uniform in their condemnation of abortion once the fetus was considered to be a "person."

Many in the ancient and medieval world were influenced by Aristotle's beliefs regarding the time when this occurred. If they could know what we know about the fetus from its earliest stages of life, I believe they would revise their opinion and condemn abortion from the moment of conception. But it is impossible to know their position on information they did not possess.

WHAT ABOUT RAPE AND INCEST?

The Bible makes rape a capital offense: "If the man meets the engaged woman in the open country, and the man seizes her and lies with her, then only the man who lay with her shall die. You shall do nothing to the young woman; the young woman has not committed an offense punishable by death, because this case is like that of someone who attacks and murders a neighbor" (Deuteronomy 22:25–26).

God's word clearly condemns such a crime against women. "Pro-choice" advocates often point to this issue early in the debate, arguing that a woman should not continue to be victimized by bearing a child as the result of such a horrific crime.

Unprotected intercourse results in pregnancy about four percent of the time. If one in three women is likely to be raped in her lifetime, and incestuous relationships subject a woman to repeated sexual abuse, pregnancies resulting from rape and incest are so likely that abortion must be legal as a remedy for women subjected to such crime. Nearly all pro-life advocates concede the point, allowing for abortion in the case of rape and incest.

However, it has been established by numerous surveys over the years that rape and incest victims represent approximately one percent of the abortion cases recorded annually in this country. A decision to limit abortions to this exception would prevent the deaths of nearly all of the 1.5 million babies who are aborted each year. Only about three percent of the abortions performed each year in America relate to the health of the mother, and three percent relate to the health of the child. Ninety-three percent are elective.

To allow for abortion because of the very rare incidence of abortions performed because of rape and incest is something like ceasing the use of traffic lights because of the incidents when they slow a sick person's rush to a hospital. Would we not cause more harm than we prevent?

At the same time, Americans must be conscious of the fact that rape and incest are far more common in some other countries and cultures. Rape in particular is a typical means of coercion and military control in some societies. There the percentage of abortions related to rape may be much higher than is the case in America.

This caveat stated, I'm not sure that even this decision is the moral choice. I won't pretend to understand what it's like for women who have experienced such trauma as rape and incest. But it is hard for me to understand how the child which is produced by this terrible crime does not deserve to live.

Ethel Waters, the famous gospel singer, was the product of a rape. So was a student I taught at Southwestern Seminary, an evangelist with a global ministry today. I tread very lightly here, but would at the very least suggest that this issue is far from the primary cause of abortion in America today.

A WAY FORWARD IN PRO-LIFE VS. PRO-CHOICE

"Pro-life" advocates typically believe that life begins at conception, meaning abortion at any stage of the pregnancy is taking a human life. "Pro-choice" advocates typically belief that life begins when the fetus is viable independent of its mother or at birth, and that abortion should be a legal choice for the mother prior to that point. The framers of the Constitution did not address this issue. The Supreme Court in 1973 interpreted this silence to mean that constitutional rights to life do not extend to the preborn. And yet the Bible speaks with a single voice in viewing the preborn as the creation of God and as children deserving of protection and care.

In light of these contradictory facts, is there a way to move forward?

Given that the participants in this debate come from a variety of religious and personal worldviews, it seems implausible to find common ground by beginning with biblical teachings or religious convictions. So I suggest the following non-religious, constitutional strategy.

First, we should build a consensus for permitting abortion to protect the life of the mother or in cases of rape and incest.

These account for a small percentage of the 1.5 million abortions performed each year. Even though some (like me) question the morality of this position, most would concede the point in order to reduce the 93 percent of abortions which are elective in nature. Allowing for this exception removes the most obvious and emotional obstacle to the "pro-life" position. Moreover, it does not prevent us from advocating for the child's life through counseling and ministering to the victims of rape and incest who are considering abortion.

Second, we should understand that the preborn possess at least the potential for "life," however it is defined.

Many of us believe that a fetus is a human being by every definition of the term except independent viability, and note that the preborn will attain this status unless harmed. But even those who disagree with this assertion will admit that every fetus is in the process of becoming a "person."

Third, "pro-life" and "pro-choice" advocates should work together to fulfill former president Bill Clinton's desire that abortion be "rare." There was a time not long ago when this was considered the progressive position, and the vast majority of "pro-choice" supporters are likely willing to work toward an agenda intended to decrease the number of abortions performed each year.

One way to achieve this goal would be for both sides to promote adoption as the best answer to an unwanted pregnancy. Both sides could also support birth control education. Many "pro-life" advocates view birth control measures as promoting sexual promiscuity, but we may have to choose between sexual activity or unintended pregnancy and a resulting abortion.

Both sides could join forces in educating the public about the actual characteristics of the fetus. It has been proven that women are far less likely to choose abortion when they see a sonogram of their unborn child or learn about its present capacities. Adoption would then become a more likely option for the mother to choose. Leaders from both sides could be asked to adopt a united agenda aimed at decreasing the number of abortions performed each year in our country. If this strategy is successful, it may change the public's opinion regarding the morality of abortion.

Fourth, whatever the "pro-choice" position decides to do to help limit abortions, "pro-life" advocates must do all we can to care for both the unborn child and its mother.

We must care for the mother and the father of the child, and do all we can to help those who have chosen abortion in the past. We must work hard to advocate adoption and to provide life necessities for at-risk families. A great deal of common ground exists for both sides to work together in improving and caring for those considering abortion. We must be "pro-life," not just "pro-birth," and by shifting the conversation beyond abortion to the larger issues that often drive mothers and fathers toward that decision, we can help people see beyond the stereotypes that so often stigmatize those on both sides.

It may be that these steps would eventually help to change the legal status of abortion. However, even if they don't, the most effective way to save the lives of the unborn will always be to change the minds of those considering abortion, and we don't need the government to do that.

CHOOSE LIFE

Mother Teresa, writing to the US Supreme Court as it was considering petitions related to the abortion issue, stated boldly:

> Your opinion [in Roe v. Wade] stated that you did not need to "resolve the difficult question of when life begins." That question is inescapable. If the right to life is an inherent and inalienable right, it must surely obtain wherever human life exists. No one can deny that the unborn child is a distinct being, that it is human, and that it is alive. It is unjust, therefore, to deprive the unborn child of its fundamental right to life on the basis of its age, size, or condition of dependency. It was a sad infidelity to America's highest ideals when this Court said that it did not matter, or could not be determined, when the inalienable right to life began for a child in its mother's womb.

She has been widely quoted as stating, "It is a poverty to decide that a child must die so that you may live as you wish."

I attended my first National Prayer Breakfast in 1995, where I heard remarkable speakers address the president and other national leaders. Those attending were still talking about the previous year's keynote speaker. Mother Teresa, eighty-three years old in 1994, had said to the three thousand in the audience, "I feel that the greatest destroyer of peace today is abortion, because it is a war against the child, a direct killing of the innocent child, murder by the mother herself. And if we accept that a mother can kill even her own child, how can we tell other people not to kill one another?" Later in her speech she implored the gathering, "Please don't kill the child. I want the child. Please give me the child."

She received a standing ovation. After her speech, she approached President Clinton, pointed her finger at him, and said, "Stop killing babies."

Would abortion be a moral choice when a family is very, very poor—when they have fourteen children and another on the way?

That child was John Wesley.

What about a father who is ill and a mother with tuberculosis? Their first child is blind, the second is deceased, the third is deaf, and the fourth has tuberculosis. Now she is pregnant again.

Her son would be called Beethoven.

A white man rapes a thirteen-year-old black girl and she becomes pregnant.

Her child is Ethel Waters.

A teenage girl is pregnant, but her fiancée is not the father of the baby.

Her baby is Jesus.

In a church I once pastored, a woman gave me her unsolicited testimony regarding an abortion she had chosen eleven years earlier. Here's her story:

> I cried tears of shame, tears of pain, tears of heartache. I cried for my sin so black I didn't believe that there could ever be a way that I could make amends–ever be a way that I could atone for what I had done. That there could ever be a way that I could be clean again. For 11 years I cried for myself, because I couldn't get away from what I had done.
>
> But God blessed me. In the depths of my dark and lonely valley he was there. His grace and mercy are great–his love is so wonderful. He wooed me back to his side, saying to me, My child, my child, I love you. O my child I love you. Yes, I forgive you.
>
> I am blessed. I know that I am forgiven. I have forgiven myself–God has healed me. But many are not so blessed–they never get to meet my Jesus; they never experience his love and forgiveness. For them, the crying goes on.

A DISCUSSION GUIDE ON ABORTION

The following discussion guide may be used in a small group setting or for your personal time of devotion.

We hope it helps you both better understand the topic and how God might want to use you, in your specific context, to be "salt and light" on this issue.

1. What is your stance on abortion? What views does your local community hold on abortion?

2. I state that "abortion is the moral issue of our time." Do you agree? Why or why not?

3. Review the four arguments that have developed since 1973 regarding when abortion should be permissible.

    - There should be no right to an abortion, even to save the life of the mother. This has been the Catholic Church's usual position.

    - Therapeutic abortions can be performed to save the mother's life.

    - Extreme case abortions can be permitted in cases of rape, incest, or severe deformation of the fetus. Most pro-life advocates would accept therapeutic and extreme case abortions.

    - Abortion should be available to any woman who chooses it.

    Which of the statements seems most reasonable and why?

4. Review the five moral arguments for pro-choice:

    1. No one can say when a fetus becomes a person, so the mother is the most appropriate person to make decisions regarding it.

    2. Abortion must be protected so a woman who is the victim of rape or incest does not have to bear a child resulting from such an attack.

    3. No unwanted child should be brought into the world.

    4. The state has no right to legislate personal morality.

    5. A woman must be permitted to make pregnancy decisions in light of her life circumstances.

    Have you ever entered into a discussion or debate with someone regarding these statements? If so, how did you respond? I expound on the five arguments. To what extent do you empathize with my reasoning?

5. Read the following pro-life arguments listed in the article.

    - A fetus is a human life and should be granted the full protection of the law.
    - Most pro-life advocates are willing to permit abortion in cases of rape or incest or to protect the life of the mother.

- Pro-life advocates agree that all children should be wanted, so they argue strongly for adoption as an alternative to abortion.
- Pro-life supporters do not see abortion legislation as an intrusion into areas of private morality.
- Pro-life advocates want to encourage the health of both the mother and the child and do not believe that we must choose between the two.

Does one argument stand out to you as particularly significant? If so, why? Do you disagree with any of the statements? Do Christians act honorably when standing for these principles? If so, how? If not, how can Christian communities better show their pro-life support?

6. Consider the following approaches to the question "When does life begin"?

    - Functionalism: A fetus is a "person" when it can act personally as a moral, intellectual, and spiritual agent.
    - Actualism: A fetus is a person if it possesses the potential for developing self-conscious, personal life. This definition would permit abortion when the fetus clearly does not possess the capacity for functional life.
    - Essentialism: A fetus is a person from conception, whatever its health or potential. It is an individual in the earliest stages of development and deserves all the protections afforded to other persons by our society.

    Which approach seems most biblical? Why?

7. Why is our answer as Christians to the question "When does life begin?" so important?

8. What Christian teaching have you heard on abortion? Do these use specific Bible passages? If so, which ones?

9. Of the important passages highlighted in this essay, which for you best explains the biblical stance of life in the womb? (Exodus 21:22, Genesis 2:7, Psalm 139, Jeremiah 1:5, Luke 1:39–45). Which of these passages is most shocking to you, if any?

10. Do you think that mothers who have been raped should be able to opt for abortion? If so, why?

11. In "A way forward in pro-life vs. pro-choice," I write that Christians should:

    - One: build a consensus for permitting abortion to protect the life of the mother or in cases of rape and incest.

    - Two: understand that the preborn possess at least the potential for "life," however it is defined.

    - Three: "Pro-life" and "pro-choice" advocates should work together to fulfill President Clinton's desire that abortion be "rare."

    - Four: whatever the "pro-choice" position decides to do to help limit abortions, "pro-life" advocates must do all we can to care for both the unborn child and its mother.

Are the points straightforward, or is there room for disagreement? Which of the points resonated most with you? Are there any you would add to the list?

12. Reread the testimony given at the end of the article. In our local communities, how can we better serve women considering abortion or women who have already had one?

13. Does knowing that so many of the "greats" in history were unwanted pregnancies shift your perspective on abortion?

14. Have any of your views been changed or altered after reading this article? If so, how?

7
THE GREATEST SIN IN AMERICA

What does the Bible say about racism?

In 2019, Pew Research Center reported that "a majority of Americans say race relations in the United States are bad, and of those, about seven-in-ten say things are getting even worse." And those trends have continued in the years since.

A generation after the 1954 Brown school desegregation decision, the Civil Rights Act of 1964, and the Voting Rights Act of 1965, racial discrimination continues in our country. According to the FBI, nearly 60 percent of hate crimes are motivated by race, ethnicity, or ancestry.

RACISM AND INDIGENOUS AMERICANS

The Oxford English Dictionary defines racism as "prejudice, discrimination, or antagonism directed against someone of a different race based on the belief that one's own race is superior."

By this definition, mistreating people of a particular race is "racism" to the degree that the perpetrator considers his or her victims to be racially inferior. We find such attitudes on the part of Anglos toward non-Anglos since Europeans first landed in the New World.

Many European explorers characterized the indigenous peoples they encountered as "heathen" and considered their race and culture to be inferior by nature. Many claimed that such people could be transformed by the introduction of Christianity and European customs.

One colonist described native Americans as "having little of Humanitie but shape, ignorant of Civilitie, of Arts, of Religion; more brutish than the beasts they hunt, more wild and unmanly than the unmanned wild Countrey, which they range rather than inhabite; captivated also to Satans tyranny in foolish pieties, mad impieties, wicked idlenesse, busie and bloudy wickednesse."

RACISM AND AFRICANS

Many who supported the enslavement of Africans likewise viewed them as inferior to White people. An Anglican minister in Barbados claimed that "Negro's were Beasts, and had no more Souls than Beasts." Africans were considered intellectually and morally inferior to Whites; some declared that they were descended from apes. Such horrific claims were used to justify the system of chattel slavery (the personal ownership of a slave) that enslaved millions of Africans. Many slaveholders convinced themselves that slaves, due to their supposedly inferior nature, were better off and better cared for in bondage than in freedom.

This racist ideology led directly to America's "original sin," the institution of slavery in the New World. The first group of African slaves—four men and women—arrived at Jamestown, Virginia, in 1619. Planters quickly realized that enormous profits could be gained from importing enslaved laborers.

Africans could be made to work much longer and harder in the fields. Since they were so far from Africa, they could not easily escape and return home. In addition, African slaves came from a variety of nations and cultures and thus could not easily communicate with each other to organize resistance.

Most slaves came from West Africa, where some tribal leaders were willing to capture and sell other Africans for profit. Slaves became especially important to the economy of the South, where the climate and topography were more suitable for tobacco and cotton plantations.

By 1860, the United States was divided into "slave" and "free" states. That year, census takers counted 3,950,540 slaves in America.

While the Declaration of Independence claimed that "all men are created equal," the US Constitution determined that enslaved persons would be counted as "three-fifths of all other Persons" for purposes of government representation and taxation (Article I, Section II, Paragraph III).

The Constitution permitted importing slaves until 1808, with a tax of $10 per slave (Article I, Section IX, Clause I). And it required those living in free states to return escaped slaves to their owners (Article IV, Section II, Clause III).

Slavery was legal in America until 1865 and the adoption of the Thirteenth Amendment. The Fourteenth Amendment (1868) guaranteed the same rights to all male citizens; the Fifteenth Amendment (1870) made it illegal to deprive any eligible citizen of the right to vote, regardless of color.

However, segregation in schools was not made illegal until Brown v. Board of Education in 1954. Jim Crow laws enforcing racial segregation were overturned by the Civil Rights Act of 1964 and the Voting Rights Act of 1965.

RACISM AND ASIANS

Asian immigrants have faced racial prejudice in the US as well. Those who came to America to work in mines, farms, and railroads were willing to accept lower wages, which enraged White residents.

As a result, Asians became the victims of riots and attacks. The 1882 Chinese Exclusion Act and the 1924 Asian Exclusion Act barred additional immigration. These acts also declared Asians ineligible for citizenship, which meant they could not own land.

During World War II, President Franklin D. Roosevelt established interment camps for people of Japanese descent—including American citizens—in response to the attacks on Pearl Harbor. The stated goal was to prevent espionage during the war but, to justify their actions, military and political leaders like General John L. Dewitt knowingly filed false reports with fabricated claims of sabotage.

And while war-time efforts can be seen in a different light than racist actions during times of relative peace, it's telling that similar plans were drawn up for the internment of Italians and Germans within the country's borders before being shelved because people were less willing to entertain the idea of arresting Americans of European descent solely because of their heritage.

RACISM TODAY

Studies show that racism persists in America:

- People with "black-sounding names" had to send out 50 percent more job applications than people with "white-sounding names" to get a callback.
- A Black man is three times more likely to be searched at a traffic stop and six times more likely to go to jail than a White man.
- If a Black person kills a White person, he or she is twice as likely to receive the death sentence as a White person who kills a Black person.
- Black people serve up to 20 percent more time in prison than White people for the same crimes.
- Black people are 38 percent more likely to be sentenced to death than White people for the same crimes.
- Racism persists in America's churches as well:
- Only 32 percent of White pastors strongly agree that "my church is involved with racial reconciliation at the local level." Fifty-three percent of African American pastors strongly agree with this statement.
- Only 56 percent of evangelicals believe that "people of color are often put at a social disadvantage because of their race." Eighty-four percent of Black people agree with this statement.
- A recent study showed that 81 percent of America's Protestant churches are composed of one predominant racial group.

- While 90 percent of Protestant pastors say their congregation would welcome a sermon on racial reconciliation, only 26 percent say leaders in their church have encouraged them to preach on the subject.

Dr. Martin Luther King Jr. was right: Sunday morning worship services are still the most segregated hour in America.

SLAVERY IN THE BIBLE

When my family moved to Atlanta in 1994, we quickly fell in love with the Old South. Being from Texas, I thought something was historical if it happened while Tom Landry was coach of the Cowboys. Southern history goes back to the Revolutionary War and colonial times. I was especially fascinated by the Civil War.

But there's a dark side to the story. While traveling one day in the beautiful city of Charleston, South Carolina, my wife and I came upon a "slave-trading warehouse." This was the horrific place where slaves were brought to America on ships and then sold at market in chains.

I can still remember the crumbling limestone building and my revulsion upon seeing it. I believe that racism is the greatest sin in America, the failure which keeps us from addressing our other failures. Racism makes crime in south Dallas a "Black" problem and drug abuse in north Dallas a "White" problem when they're both our problems.

Given our tragic history with racism, thinking about the subject of slavery in the Bible is a bit repugnant for most of us. However, since many say the Bible was wrong on this issue, we must discuss this painful subject briefly.

Slavery in the Old Testament

It is an unfortunate fact that slavery was an accepted part of life in the ancient world. No early society or literature questioned its existence or necessity.

People in Old Testament times became slaves in a variety of ways: they were born to enslaved parents (Genesis 17:23), purchased as slaves (Genesis 37:28), or sold themselves to pay a debt (Leviticus 25:39–55). Breaking into a home was punished by enslavement (Exodus 22:3), and prisoners of war were commonly enslaved (Joel 3:6). The children of Israel enslaved the Canaanites they conquered in the Promised Land (Judges 1:28).

Slaves in Israel were considered property to be bought and sold (Exodus 21:32). However, they were granted protection against murder, permanent injury, or undue physical labor (Exodus 21:20, 26; 23:12). Hebrew household slaves were included at religious meals (Exodus 12:44). Such privileges and protections were extremely rare in the ancient world.

But why did the Old Testament not condemn this practice?

In many ways, it did. There were several ways a Hebrew slave could be freed (a process called "manumission"). An individual could be purchased and set free (Exodus 21:8). A slave permanently injured by his master was to be set free (Exodus 21:26). Hebrews were to be held as slaves for no longer than six years (Deuteronomy 15:12). The Jubilee Year, which occurred every forty-nine years, was to free all Israelite slaves (Leviticus 25:50).

But still we ask: Why did the Old Testament sanction this practice at all? Its rules minimized this evil, protected slaves from physical harm, and provided for their eventual freedom. But the New Testament gives us God's complete word on the subject.

Slavery in the New Testament

In the Old Testament era, people were enslaved primarily through war. But in the first century AD, the procreation of slaves swelled their numbers enormously. And many people actually sold themselves into slavery to improve their lives.

Owning and using people as slaves was so common in the Roman Empire that not a single Roman writer condemned the practice. But this acceptance of slavery would begin to change with the growth and influence of Christianity. Slavery in the Roman era was dramatically different from the despicable practice in American history. If you walked through any first-century Roman city, you would not be able to tell most slaves from free people. Slaves performed manual labor, but they were also doctors, nurses, household managers, and intellectuals. They managed finances and cities. They were often given an excellent education at the expense of their owners, with the result that philosophers and tutors were typically slaves.

Even more amazing to us, it was common for people to sell themselves into slavery to secure such privileges. A person who wanted to be a Roman citizen could sell himself to a citizen and then purchase his freedom. For many people, slavery was more a process than a condition.

While there is no doubt that many slaves were abused physically, sexually, and socially, many were part of the more privileged strata of society. The total dependence of the Roman economy upon the labor of slaves made it impossible for the ancient world to conceive of abolishing this institution. If an economist were to propose that we refuse all goods and services imported from outside America, we'd be equally surprised.

As a result, no New Testament writer attempted to end slavery itself, as this was not possible in their time. But several other facts should be noted as well.

One: Paul abolished all racial and social discrimination for Christians: "In Christ Jesus you are all sons of God, through faith. For as many of you as were baptized into Christ have put on Christ. There is neither Jew nor Greek, there is neither slave nor free, there is no male and female, for you are all one in Christ Jesus" (Galatians 3:26–28).

Every believer is our sister or brother. None in the Christian family are to be viewed as slaves.

Two: Free Christians viewed slaves as their equal.

Paul appealed to Philemon to see his slave, Onesimus, "no longer as a bondservant but more than a bondservant, as a beloved brother" (Philemon 16).

Clement, a friend of Paul, wrote in his letter to the Corinthians (ca. AD 90), "We know many among ourselves who have given themselves up to bonds, in order that they might ransom others. Many, too, have surrendered themselves to slavery, that with the price which they received for themselves, they might provide food for others" (ch. 55). Ignatius (died AD 107) wrote to Polycarp: "Do not despise either male or female slaves, yet neither let them be puffed up with conceit, but rather let them submit themselves the more, for the glory of God, that they may obtain from God a better liberty."

Three: The New Testament church gave those who were enslaved a family and a home.

This was one reason why so many of the earliest believers were slaves. Pastors and church leaders came from the ranks both of slaves and free. Christians made no distinction between the two, for their Father welcomed all as his children.

Four: Not a single New Testament leader owned slaves, even though many had the resources to purchase them.

Their example inspired William Wilberforce and countless other Christians to do all they could to abolish slavery, and we thank God that they were successful.

RACISM AND THE BIBLE

The Bible clearly condemns all forms of racism and views every person as equally valuable. Let's look at what God's word says about our subject, then we'll consider common questions people ask about the Scriptures and racism.

Six theological facts

One: We are all created by God.

The human story begins in Genesis 1, where God "created man in his own image, in the image of God he created him; male and female he created them" (v. 27). Every person is created intentionally by God in his own divine image. Thus, every person is sacred and equally valuable. Every form of racism, by definition, is to be rejected.

Two: We are all descended from the same parents.

Every human being is descended from Adam and Eve (Genesis 1:28). As a result, "The man called his wife's name Eve, because she was the mother of all living" (Genesis 3:20).

As Scripture notes, the Lord "made from one man every nation of mankind to live on all the face of the earth" (Acts 17:26). Because of the Flood, all of humanity can trace our ancestry to Noah as well (Genesis 9:1).

Three: Every person is equally valuable to God.

As noted earlier, Paul stated boldly: "There is neither Jew nor Greek, there is neither slave nor free, there is no male and female, for you are all one in Christ Jesus" (Galatians 3:28). This at a time when many Jews considered Greeks to be unclean and inferior. Some claimed that God made Gentiles so there would be "firewood in hell." Many refused even to look upon a Gentile in public.

For their part, Gentiles persecuted the Jewish people across nearly their entire history. The Jews were enslaved by Egypt, attacked by Canaanites and other surrounding tribes, destroyed by Assyria, enslaved by Babylon, and ruled by Persia, Greece, and Rome. The Roman Empire destroyed their temple in AD 70 and disbanded their nation after the Bar Kochba revolt in AD 132–135. Nonetheless, Scripture teaches that "there is neither Jew nor Greek" in the eyes of God.

"There is neither slave nor free" was also a revolutionary claim. As we have seen, slavery was endemic in the first-century world. Many viewed slaves, especially those who came from foreign lands, as inferior to Romans.

"There is no male and female" was a radical statement as well. Romans considered women to be the possession of men. A female belonged to her father until she belonged to her husband. Women were either wives or concubines, with few rights of their own.

Galatians 3:28 sounds the clarion call that every form of racism known to Paul's day was invalid and sinful. The God who made us all loves us all.

Paul repeated his assertion to the Colossians: "There is not Greek and Jew, circumcised and uncircumcised, barbarian, Scythian, slave, free; but Christ is all, and in all" (Colossians 3:11).

To summarize: "God shows no partiality" (Acts 10:34).

Four: Each person is equally welcome to salvation in Christ.

God loves all sinners and wants all to come to faith in his Son: "God shows his love for us in that while we were still sinners, Christ died for us" (Romans 5:8). Our Lord "is patient toward you, not wishing that any should perish, but that all should reach repentance" (2 Peter 3:9).

As Paul noted, God "desires all people to be saved and to come to the knowledge of the truth" (1 Timothy 2:4). That's why the apostle could testify: "I am not ashamed of the gospel, for it is the power of God for salvation to everyone who believes, to the Jew first and also to the Greek" (Romans 1:16).

Our Father's saving love is available to all: "There is no distinction between Jew and Greek; for the same Lord is Lord of all, bestowing his riches on all who call on him" (Romans 10:12). His grace is universal: "For God so loved the world, that he gave his only Son, that whoever believes in him should not perish but have eternal life" (John 3:16).

When we trust in Christ, we become one people: "He himself is our peace, who has made us both one and has broken down in his flesh the dividing wall of hostility" (Ephesians 2:14). As a result, "In one Spirit we were all baptized into one body—Jews or Greeks, slaves or free—and all were made to drink of one Spirit" (1 Corinthians 12:13).

Jesus "is the propitiation for our sins, and not for ours only but also for the sins of the whole world" (1 John 2:2). Peter told his fellow Jewish Christians that God "made no distinction between [Gentile Christians] and us, having cleansed their hearts by faith" (Acts 15:9). As a result, we are to "make disciples of all nations" (Matthew 28:19). "Nations" translates ethnos, meaning people groups. We get "ethnicity" from this word. Every person of every ethnicity is to be brought to Christ through the ministry of the church.

Five: All people will be equally valuable in paradise.

John was given this vision of heaven: "After this I looked, and behold, a great multitude that no one could number, from every nation, from all tribes and peoples and languages, standing before the throne and before the Lamb, clothed in white robes, with palm branches in their hands" (Revelation 7:9).

Six: We are to love all people unconditionally.

God's word is blunt: "If you show partiality, you are committing sin and are convicted by the law as transgressors" (James 2:9). "Partiality" translates *prosopolempsia*, meaning to show favoritism or prejudice, to treat one person as inherently better than another. Such prejudice is "sin."

God told his people: "You shall treat the stranger who sojourns with you as the native among you, and you shall love him as yourself, for you were strangers in the land of Egypt" (Leviticus 19:34).

Jesus taught us: "Whatever you wish that others would do to you, do also to them, for this is the Law and the Prophets" (Matthew 7:12). We are to "love your neighbor as yourself" (Matthew 22:39, quoting Leviticus 19:18).

Peter testified to the Gentiles who sought to hear the gospel: "You yourselves know how unlawful it is for a Jew to associate with or to visit anyone of another nation, but God has shown me that I should not call any person common or unclean" (Acts 10:28). And that command remains a standard to which the Lord holds his people today as well.

THREE COMMON QUESTIONS

One: What about the "mark of Cain"?

After Cain murdered his brother, God sentenced him to be "a fugitive and a wanderer on the earth" (Genesis 4:12). Cain protested that "I shall be a fugitive and a wanderer on the earth, and whoever finds me will kill me" (v. 14).

God replied, "Not so! If anyone kills Cain, vengeance shall be taken on him sevenfold'" (v. 15a). Then, "the LORD put a mark on Cain, lest any who found him should attack him" (v. 15b).

The Hebrew word translated "mark" is *ot*, referring to a sign or token. It is used eighty times in the Old Testament; not once does it refer to skin color. Nonetheless, some have identified this "mark" with being Black. Since Cain was cursed for his sin against his brother, it was claimed that those whose skin was black were his descendants and were cursed by God. This claim was used to justify the enslavement of Africans.

This line of reasoning is completely wrong. As noted, the "mark" of Cain had nothing to do with his skin color. In addition, Cain's family line probably died in the Flood.

And note that Moses married a "Cushite woman" (Numbers 12:1). Cush was a region south of Ethiopia; its people were known for their black skin (Jeremiah 13:23). When Moses' brother and sister spoke against him for marrying his Cushite wife, God rebuked them, even turning Miriam stark white with leprosy for a time as a public sign of his displeasure (Numbers 12:4–15).

Clearly, the "mark of Cain" has nothing to do with Black people.

Two: What about the "curse of Ham"?

Ham was one of Noah's three sons. Ham had four sons: Cush, Egypt, Put, and Canaan (Genesis 10:6). Ham is considered the father of Black people, since some of his descendants settled in Africa.

According to tradition, Cush settled in Ethiopia, south of Egypt; Egypt (also known as "Mizraim") settled in the land of Egypt; Put settled in Libya; Canaan settled above Africa and east of the Mediterranean Sea.

The Bible tells us that after the Flood, Noah became drunk (Genesis 9:21). Then "Ham, the father of Canaan, saw the nakedness of his father and told his two brothers outside" (v. 22). Shem and Japheth "covered the nakedness of their father" (v. 23). After Noah awoke, he said, "Cursed be Canaan; a servant of servants shall he be to his brothers" (v. 25).

Note that Noah cursed Canaan, not Ham. Thus, his curse was irrelevant to Ham's sons who had settled in Africa and their descendants.

Also note that Noah's curse was specifically directed at Canaan, with no mention of his descendants. If Noah's curse was applied to his descendants, it related to the Canaanites living in the land that became Israel. It had nothing whatever to do with Black people.

Nonetheless, the Old Scofield Reference Bible of 1909 (often considered the authoritative Bible of fundamentalist Christians) interprets Genesis 9:24–25 to teach: "A prophetic declaration is made that from Ham will descend an inferior and servile posterity."

With his typically brilliant exposition, Dr. Tony Evans addresses this issue, noting that biblical curses are limited to three or four generations (Exodus 20:5) and are reversed when people repent and return to obedience (Exodus 20:6). As Dr. Evans shows, Scripture consistently rebukes and rejects the claim that Black people (or any other race) are inferior to any other.

Three: Didn't slavery proponents use the Bible to justify their position?

Tragically, many who supported slavery in the antebellum South used the "mark of Cain" and "curse of Ham" to justify their position. They also noted biblical statements encouraging slaves to obey their masters.

As we saw in the section on slavery, the Bible deals realistically with the practice where necessary, but it clearly endorses the intrinsic sacred value of each person. The biblical emphasis on the sanctity of life was one of the key motivating factors for William Wilberforce and others who worked so sacrificially to abolish slavery.

Like any other book, the Bible can be misused by those who misinterpret and misrepresent its teachings. For instance, when chloroform was developed, some were resistant to using it for women in childbirth since Genesis 3:16 teaches "in pain you shall bring forth children."

When oil wells were first dug in Pennsylvania, many New York ministers opposed the project on the grounds that it would deplete the oil stored for the predestined burning of the world (2 Peter 3:10, 12).

And winnowing fans were rejected by Christians who thought they interfered with the providence of God since "the wind blows where it wishes" (John 3:8). (For these and other examples, see John P. Newport and William Cannon, *Why Christians Fight Over the Bible.*)

When a doctor misuses medicine, we blame the physician, not the science. When an attorney misrepresents a legal statute, we blame the lawyer, not the law.

In responding to racists who misused the Bible to justify slavery, we should blame the racists, not the word of God.

PRACTICAL RESPONSES

God's word clearly calls us to love every person as unconditionally as he loves us.

How do we put such love into practice today?

One: Search your own heart

A recent survey reported that 83 percent of Americans consider racism to still be a problem in our society and politics. Notably, not a single Black responder in the poll said that racism was no longer an issue.

Why is racism so pervasive and perennial in our culture?

C. S. Lewis wrote that "if anyone would like to acquire humility, I can, I think, tell him the first step. The first step is to realize that one is proud. And a biggish step, too. At least, nothing whatever can be done before it. If you think you are not conceited, it means you are very conceited indeed."

I think his logic applies to the issue of racism as well.

One reason racial discrimination is such a perennial problem is that it appeals to the core of our sin nature. In the Garden of Eden, the serpent promised the woman that if she ate of the forbidden fruit, "you will be like God" (Genesis 3:5).

From then to now, our desire to be our own god is at the root of all our sin. As Friedrich Nietzsche noted, the "will to power" is the basic drive in human nature.

Here's my point: Racism is a way to feel superior to others on the basis of immutable realities. If I'm White and you're Black, I will always be White and you will always be Black. If I delude myself into believing that being White is superior to being Black, I will therefore always feel superior to you.

This temptation is alluring on levels we often don't recognize. In fact, I think Satan wants us not to acknowledge our discriminatory inclinations, lest we admit and repent of them.

And note that this temptation is part of our fallen humanity rather than restricted to any one particular race. Every person, regardless of background and skin color, is capable of the racism that Scripture condemns. So every person needs to be wary of this sin becoming an issue in his or her life.

It is therefore a good first step in confronting racism to check ourselves. Ask the Holy Spirit to show you any unstated attitudes or assumptions that are discriminatory. Ask him to reveal to you any thoughts, words, or actions that are racist.

Pray regularly for such discernment. And where necessary, repent.

Two: Take the cultural initiative

"In some ways, it's super simple. People learn to be whatever their society and culture teaches them. We often assume it takes parents actively teaching their kids, for them to be racist. The truth is that unless parents actively teach kids not to be racists, they will be." This is how Jennifer Richeson, a Yale University social psychologist, explains the continued pervasiveness of racism.

She continues: "This is not the product of some deep-seated, evil heart that is cultivated. It comes from the environment, the air all around us." Eric Knowles, a psychology professor at New York University, adds: "There's a lot of evidence that people have an ingrained even evolved tendency toward people who are in our so-called 'in group.'"

What is the solution? "The only way to change bias is to change culture," according to Richeson. "You have to change what is acceptable in society. People today complain about politically correct culture, but what that does is provide a check on people's outward attitude, which in turn influences how we think about ourselves internally. Everything we're exposed to gives us messages about who is good and bad." Such change starts with us. Christians are "the salt of the earth" and "the light of the world" (Matthew 5:13, 14). If food lacks salt, the fault is not with the food. If a dark room lacks light, the fault is not with the room.

You and I must set the standard in our churches, communities, and families. We must be the change we want to see. We must take proactive, positive, initiatory steps to model the inclusive love of Jesus.

Three: Be the church

On July 12, 2016, President George W. Bush spoke at a memorial service held in Dallas for police officers who had been killed in the line of duty. He made this remarkable point: "Americans, I think, have a great advantage. To renew our unity, we only need to remember our values. We have never been held together by blood or background. We are bound by things of the spirit, by shared commitments to common ideals."

President Bush is right. Many nations find their unity in a monolithic racial heritage, culture, or history. But America has never been about such uniformity. From the beginning, we were home to Protestants and Catholics and Jews, immigrants from across Europe and around the world.

As a result, our truest unity will never be horizontal, only vertical. President Bush: "At our best, we honor the image of God we see in one another. We recognize that we are brothers and sisters, sharing the same brief moment on Earth and owing each other the loyalty of our shared humanity."

In other words, the closer we draw to our Father, the closer we draw to each other.

That's why the gospel of God's reconciling love is the only transforming answer to the challenges we face. Legislation and the civil rights movement were essential to improving the lives of those who faced legalized discrimination. But laws cannot change people. Only the Spirit can do that. As a result, Christians are on the front lines of this spiritual battle for the soul and future of our nation.

Writing for *The Washington Post*, Dr. Evans traced our racial challenges "directly to ineffective Christians" and stated, "One of the real tragedies today is that the Church as a whole has not furthered God's light, equity, love and principles in our land in order to be a positive influence and impact for good in the midst of darkness, fear and hate."

He called for churches to unite in a "solemn assembly" with prayer and fasting, to train our members to be verbal and visible followers of Jesus, and to unite for good works in our communities. This is our "God-given role of influencing the conscience of our culture." Without it "our country will keep spiraling downward into the depths of fear and hate."

The time has come for the church to be the church.

CONCLUSION

Every person of every race was created by the same God in his image. Every one.

Early Christians believed this transforming truth. In the second century, Justin Martyr said of his fellow Christians:

"We who hated and destroyed one another, and on account of their different manners would not live with men of a different tribe, now, since the coming of Christ, live familiarly with them, and pray for our enemies."

Clement of Alexandria described the true Christian: "Through the perfection of his love he impoverishes himself that he may never overlook a brother in affliction, especially if he knows that he could himself bear want better than his brother."

An early Christian named Minucius Felix told the Romans, "We love one another . . . with a mutual love, because we do not know how to hate." Tertullian, a second-century theologian, reported that pagans said of Christians, "See how they love one another."

Now it's our turn.

A DISCUSSION GUIDE ON RACISM

The following discussion guide may be used in a small group setting or for your personal time of devotion. We hope it helps you both better understand the topic and how God might want to use you, in your specific context, to be "salt and light" on this issue.

1. What is the most recent race-related death you've read or seen in the news?
2. How did your family or friends respond to that news?
3. How did you respond?
4. Why is it important to know the history of racism in America?
5. Considering racism in the church, how can your church increase its diversity?
6. Recall Martin Luther King Jr.'s famous quote that Sunday morning worship services are the most segregated hour in America. When that is the case, is it necessarily the result of racism? Can you think of any alternative reasons why Sunday morning worship services might be predominantly one race? What are some ways churches that are not multiracial can partner with other Christians to model the diversity of God's kingdom?
7. "Racism makes crime in south Dallas a 'Black' problem and drug abuse in north Dallas a 'White' problem when they're both our problems." What's the problem with designating social issues to certain races?
8. Before reading this chapter, what did you know about slavery in the Bible?

9. The conceptions and reality of slavery in the Bible are different from those of slavery in America's history. Recall the following important biblical events/statements against slavery in the New Testament:
    - Paul abolished all racial and social discrimination for Christians.
    - Free Christians viewed slaves as their equal.
    - The New Testament church gave those who were enslaved a family and a home.
    - Not a single New Testament leader owned slaves, even though many had the resources to purchase them.
    - Which points stand out to you? Why? Note the biblical references in this chapter. What do these biblical truths tell you about the early church? How do their practices inform our ideas of church today?

10. Do any of the six theological facts in the subsection "Racism and the Bible" stand out to you as particularly significant? If so, why?

11. Why is it important that we base our beliefs about community on these theological facts?

12. Were you aware of the arguments of the mark of Cain and the curse of Ham before reading this chapter? Do you agree or disagree with the stance taken in this chapter? Why?

13. "In responding to racists who misused the Bible to justify slavery, we should blame the racists, not the word of God." Why is this an important distinction?

14. Why is searching our hearts such a necessary and "good first step"?

15. In your local community, how can you actively seek to change culture?

16. Why is it important that we continually return to God and his truth when we think about aspects of community?

17. How can you make loving others more of a priority in your life?

8

THE CALL TO TRANSFORMATIONAL GOOD

What does the Bible say about politics and religious liberty?

William Wilberforce experienced a spiritual rebirth on Easter 1786 that led him to discover his life's purpose. As he wrote later in his diary, "My walk is a public one. My business is in the world, and I must mix in the assemblies of men or quit the post which Providence seems to have assigned me."

He soon came to see the horrors of the English slave trade and became so convicted that he wrote, "Let the consequences be what they would: I from this time determined that I would never rest until I had effected its absolution." He was vilified by pro-slavery forces and blocked repeatedly in Parliament. However, the persistent and sacrificial efforts of Wilberforce and his associates finally led to the abolishing of the slave trade and slavery in the British Empire. Historian G. M. Trevelyan later called this "one of the turning events in the history of the world." As Wilberforce's story illustrates, God can use Christians in politics for profound and transformational good.

Merriam-Webster defines "politics" as "the art or science of government." The word comes from the Greek *polis*, meaning "city." It has its roots in Aristotle's classic work, *Politika*, which introduced the Greek term *politika*, meaning "affairs of the cities."

Anthropologists generally recognize four kinds of political systems:

1. **The band**: a small family group consisting of no more than thirty to fifty individuals.

2. **The tribe**: a group consisting of many families with social institutions such as chiefs or elders. They are more permanent than bands.

3. **The chiefdom**: more complex than a tribe or a band society, they have a centralized authority structure and institutional leadership.

4. **The sovereign state**: a state with a permanent population, a defined territory, a government, and the capacity to relate to other sovereign states.

For the purposes of this chapter, we will focus on biblical insights with regard to the "sovereign state" of the United States. What insights can help Christians relate more effectively to our culture as salt and light? How can we make a difference in the culture and act in ways that empower our witness?

Let's consider two biblical facts before pivoting to how those points are crucial to understanding and using the religious liberty we are blessed to have in the United States.

GOD CALLS AND USES POLITICAL LEADERS

In *Nicomachean Ethics,* Aristotle observed, "the activity of the politician also is unleisured, and aims at securing something beyond the mere participation in politics—positions of authority and honor, or, if the happiness of the politician himself and of his fellow-citizens, this happiness conceived as something distinct from political activity." Russian Premier Nikita Khrushchev made a similar point: "Politicians are the same all over. They promise to build a bridge where there is no river."

It is tempting for Christians to stay "above" politics and out of the fray. In this day of "cancel culture" and 24/7 media coverage, in a nation that feels more divided and divisive than ever, it is understandable for good people to sit on the sidelines. However, as Plato noted in *The Republic*, "One of the penalties for refusing to participate in politics is that you end up being governed by your inferiors." The Bible makes clear that, despite the stigma often associated with politics, God calls and uses political leaders. Consider three dimensions of this call.

God uses leaders who partner with him

The Bible is replete with stories of political leaders called and used by God to work with him in advancing his kingdom on earth. Let's review four such examples.

One: Joseph

Joseph was sold into slavery by his brothers at the age of seventeen. Thirteen years later, he became what we might call the "prime minister" of Egypt, the world's greatest superpower. His rise to power was no accident: When he was in prison, God gave him the ability to interpret Pharaoh's dreams, thus predicting seven years of plenty followed by seven years of famine (Genesis 41:1–36). As a result, "Pharaoh said to his servants, 'Can we find a man like this, in whom is the Spirit of God?'" (v. 38).

Pharaoh then appointed Joseph to political office: "You shall be over my house, and all my people shall order themselves as you command. Only as regards the throne will I be greater than you" (v. 40). This description means Joseph was appointed as the "grand vizier" of Egypt. In this role, he was instrumental in saving the Egyptian people and his own family from starvation, preserving the Jewish nation through whom the Messiah would come one day.

Two: Israel's leaders

God called Moses to lead his people out of Egyptian slavery (Exodus 3) and then Joshua to follow next (Joshua 1:1–2). The Lord then "raised up judges, who saved [the nation] out of the hand of those who plundered them" (Judges 2:16). God later designated Saul to be Israel's first king (1 Samuel 9:15–17) and David to be his successor (1 Samuel 16:12–13).

Three: Mordecai

The book of Esther tells us about the plot of Haman against God's people in Persia. After this nefarious plot was exposed, "the king took off his signet ring, which he had taken from Haman, and gave it to Mordecai" (Esther 8:2). This action advanced Mordecai to the position of first minister of the king with authority akin to that of Joseph centuries earlier.

As a result, "Mordecai went out from the presence of the king in royal robes of blue and white, and with a great golden crown and a robe of fine linen and purple" (v. 15). Soon "the fear of Mordecai" fell on "all the officials of the provinces and the satraps and the governors and the royal agents" of the land (Esther 9:3). This was because "Mordecai was great in the king's house, and his fame spread throughout all the provinces, for the man Mordecai grew more and more powerful" (v. 4). Consequently, Mordecai's leadership enabled the Jews to defend themselves from their enemies, again preserving the nation through whom the Messiah would come.

Four: Daniel and his friends

Daniel and his friends were Jewish exiles in Babylon. Scripture says that "God gave them learning and skill in all literature and wisdom, and Daniel had understanding in all visions and dreams" (Daniel 1:17). As a result, the king elevated them to positions of political authority. Then, when Daniel (like Joseph) interpreted the king's dreams, "the king gave Daniel high honors and many great gifts, and made him ruler over the whole province of Babylon and chief prefect over all the wise men of Babylon" (Daniel 2:48).

Clearly, God calls some people into political service. We see this fact not only in Scripture but across history as well.

According to Pew Research Center, nearly all US presidents have been identified with the Christian faith. Eleven were Episcopalian; nine were Presbyterian; four were Baptist; four were Unitarian; four were Methodist; two were members of the Disciples of Christ; two were Dutch Reformed; two were Quaker; two were Catholic; one was a Congregationalist; and one was United Church of Christ. Only Andrew Johnson, Thomas Jefferson, and Abraham Lincoln had no formal church affiliation.

William Wilberforce's Christian faith led him to fight within Parliament for the abolition of the slave trade in England. Presbyterian minister John Witherspoon was the only active clergyman to sign the Declaration of Independence. Dr. Martin Luther King Jr. was a Baptist minister before he assumed political leadership of the civil rights movement.

It is clear that God calls some people into political service and uses them in this role.

God uses leaders who oppose him

Generations after Joseph's death, another Pharaoh who saw the Jewish people as a threat rose to power (Exodus 1:8–12) and "ruthlessly made the people of Israel work as slaves" (v. 13). In response, God raised up Moses to oppose Pharaoh and free his people from slavery. God then used Pharaoh's "hardened heart" to bring about the Exodus. As a result, "Israel saw the great power that the Lord used against the Egyptians, so the people feared the Lord, and they believed in the Lord and in his servant Moses" (Exodus 14:31). The Lord used King Herod's attempt to murder the baby Jesus to fulfill biblical prophecy regarding his Son's flight to Egypt (Matthew 2:13–15). He likewise used opposition from Jewish authorities in Jerusalem to bring his Son to the cross as our Savior.

After Roman magistrates in Philippi gave orders for Paul and Silas to be beaten and imprisoned (Acts 16:22–24), God redeemed their suffering by leading their jailer and his family to Christ (vv. 25–34). The Lord used opposition from a Roman government official to bring Paul to Rome

(Acts 25:12). He used Rome's exile of John to Patmos to give us the book of Revelation (cf. Revelation 1:9).

As a contemporary example, Christianity has exploded in China in the decades after Communist leaders took over in 1949. Today, China is the world's largest producer of Bibles. There are more Christians than members of the Communist Party in China. According to one scholar, "On any given Sunday, there are almost certainly more Protestants in church in China than in all of Europe."

And no one knows with certainty the size of the "underground" church in China. When I was in Beijing several years ago, I met with a group of pastors who serve such congregations. Their stories about divine protection and evangelistic multiplication read like the book of Acts.

I have been privileged to travel to Cuba ten times over the years. The spiritual awakening occurring in this Communist country is truly inspiring. On my first visit, I told one of the Cuban pastors that I was sorry for the persecution he and his people were facing and that I was praying for such opposition to lessen. He asked me not to continue with such intercession, explaining that persecution was strengthening his people and purifying their faith. Then he added that he and many other Cubans were praying for persecution to increase in the US for the same reasons.

God uses leaders who don't know they're being used

The Persian king under whom Mordecai served issued an edict stating that "the king allowed the Jews who were in every city to gather and defend their lives, to destroy, to kill, and to annihilate any armed force of any people or province that might attack them" (Esther 8:11). We have no biblical evidence that the king knew he was working to preserve God's chosen people through whom our Savior would come, but he was.

When Paul's enemies brought him before the court in Corinth, the proconsul Gallio set him free, enabling the apostle's continued ministry (Acts 18:12–16). When a riot led by idolaters broke out in Ephesus, "some of the Asiarchs, who were friends of [Paul's], sent to him and were urging him not to venture into the theater" (Acts 19:31). The "Asiarchs" were custodians of the imperial Roman cult in Asia and people of high political rank. The crowd dragged Gaius and Aristarchus, Paul's traveling companions, into the theater. However, the "town clerk" (the chief administrative officer in Ephesus) "quieted the crowd" and persuaded them to disperse (vv. 35, 41).

When Paul returned to Jerusalem, another riot broke out. However, "the tribune of the cohort" intervened (Acts 21:31). He was commander of a thousand soldiers and a person of significant authority in the city. He preserved Paul's life and enabled the furtherance of his ministry. The Jewish authorities then plotted to take Paul's life, but his nephew warned him and then brought word to the tribune. This official then provided protection for Paul and sent him along with an explanatory letter to Felix the governor in Caesarea (Acts 23:17–35).

Felix later heard Paul's case and refused to turn him over to his adversaries (Acts 24:22–23). His successor, Festus, refused a request for Paul to be returned to Jerusalem, not knowing that his enemies "were planning an ambush to kill him on the way" (Acts 25:3). Festus then honored Paul's appeal to Caesar and provided him transportation and security to Rome (Acts 27:1).

The Bible teaches that "the king's heart is a stream of water in the hand of the Lord; he turns it wherever he will" (Proverbs 21:1). No matter what circumstances seem to say, "kingship belongs to the Lord, and he rules over the nations" (Psalm 22:28). As a result, we can know that God is using leaders whether they know they are being used or not. John Calvin was right: "It is a most blessed thing to be subject to the sovereignty of God."

GOD IS CALLING US TO PARTICIPATE IN POLITICS

I have been privileged over the years to know several Christians in political leadership, both as their pastor and as their friend. One of the frequent concerns I have heard them express is the common misperception that Christians have done all they need to do if they elect Christians to office. The fact is, voting is vital, but it is just the beginning of our biblical responsibility with regard to politics.

It is true that "our citizenship is in heaven" (Philippians 3:20), but it is also true that we are to be good stewards of our time on earth. The Lord told his exiled people in Babylon: "Build houses and live in them; plant gardens and eat their produce. Take wives and have sons and daughters; take wives for your sons, and give your daughters in marriage, that they may bear sons and daughters; multiply there, and do not decrease. But seek the welfare of the city where I have sent you into exile, and pray to the Lord on its behalf, for in its welfare you will find your welfare" (Jeremiah 29:5–7).

As the "salt of the earth" and the "light of the world" (Matthew 5:13–14), the flourishing of our world is, in part, our responsibility. If I have the only light in a dark room, its darkness is my fault. Caring for our culture and engaging in its political processes is part of good citizenship for God's people. To that end, consider four practical imperatives for Christians.

Vote

Voting is an essential responsibility for all Americans and for all Christians living in democratic countries. We should learn all we can about the candidates and their positions, especially in the context of biblical principles. We should ask God to guide us in casting our ballots. The Voting Assistance Center at MyFaithVotes.org offers a wealth of helpful resources to this end, covering federal, state, and local candidates. And we should encourage everyone we can to vote as well.

How are you preparing now for your next federal, state, or local election?

Engage with legislators

One of the values of representative democracy is the degree to which our leaders are responsible to those who elect them. Several political leaders have shared with me the fact that even a few citizens who make their views known on pending legislation can make an enormous difference.

- Contact your congressional representatives. Note: it is best to speak to them or their aides personally rather than sending emails or leaving voice mails that can be ignored.

- Go to meetings organized by leaders in your community.

- Organize groups to speak with your representatives about issues important to you.

- Volunteer for candidates and causes by knocking on doors, making fundraising calls, and organizing voter registration drives.

Are you asking God to show you if and how he wants you to be involved personally in our political process?

Serve in public office

As we have seen, God calls men and women into political service and uses their work for his glory and our good. I am convinced, in fact, that God is calling more Christians into public service today than are answering his call. Have you asked God if he is calling you into such service?

Intercede

Paul's word to Timothy is God's word to us: "I urge that supplications, prayers, intercessions, and thanksgivings be made for all people, for kings and all who are in high positions" (1 Timothy 2:1–2). We are to pray for our leaders whether we agree with them or not; in fact, the less we agree, the more we should intercede. We should pray not just for the president and national leaders but for state and local leaders as well. Do you know the names of your city council? Are you praying for them and for your mayor? For your governor and state officials? For the president and his cabinet?

Participating in all four facets of political life, in accordance with God's guidance for your life, is crucial because, as the ancient Greek statesman Pericles is reported to have said, "Just because you do not take an interest in politics doesn't mean politics won't take an interest in you."

Like it or not, every one of us will be influenced by the decisions of our political leaders. As such, we can either accept those outcomes as they come or attempt to influence them in ways that honor God and further his kingdom. And in perhaps no area of culture is taking the correct approach more important than when it comes to issues of religious liberty.

PUBLIC WORSHIP AND GOVERNMENTAL AUTHORITY

In 2020, three churches in California filed a federal lawsuit against Gov. Gavin Newsom, claiming that a ban on singing in worship to help stem the spread of coronavirus violated their First Amendment rights. One explained, "Singing in church is a biblical mandate." They pointed to the governor's support of Black Lives Matter protests, claiming that he protected the protesters' freedom of expression while blocking that of Christians in worship. In their view, the governor's act constitutes a breach of their religious freedom.

The Supreme Court later ruled in their favor, deciding that the state had illegally held churches to a different standard than other public venues during the pandemic.

And while these restrictions have, for the most part, gone away since the Covid pandemic's peak, the experience has left many increasingly wary of any hints of similar overreach in the years since. As a result, questions of religious liberty and how we should relate to a government that we may not be able to trust to protect those freedoms remain at the forefront of many Christians' minds.

ARE OUR RELIGIOUS FREEDOMS UNDER ATTACK?

In *Bostock v. Clayton County*, the Supreme Court determined that LGBTQ persons must not face employment discrimination, but the court made no allowance for religious objections. However, as religious liberties legal authority David French notes, Title VII of the Civil Rights Act of 1964 "contains a provision specifically designed to protect the autonomy of religious organizations." In his view, this provision "has a profound impact on the relevant applicant pool and (along with the First Amendment) permits employers to require that applicants agree to the organization's statement of faith."

In addition, French reminds us that "religious employers are completely exempt from nondiscrimination statutes when hiring and firing 'ministerial' employees." And religious schools and similar organizations can apply for exemptions to Title IX policies regarding dorm rooms and sexual conduct when "the application of this subsection would not be consistent with the religious tenets of such organization."

In other words, religious schools and organizations after *Bostock* can still be exempt from Title IX restrictions on their religious beliefs regarding sexuality and other moral issues.

And French notes that religious organizations and schools increasingly have a right of equal access to public funds and public facilities. He adds that "the same civil rights act that now protects LGBT Americans also explicitly protects people of faith." Employees cannot be harassed because of their religious beliefs or practices or denied a reasonable accommodation of their beliefs or practices.

He adds more good news: "In the face of progressive control of the vast majority of the legal educational establishment, conservatives have created, sustained, and nurtured an intellectually vibrant and determined community of lawyers, scholars, and judges who have transformed American law to better match the meaning and text of the American Constitution. It has not accomplished all it could (what movement ever does?)—and there have been bitter disappointments—but it has made an enormous impact by securing liberties that American Christians now take for granted."

He concludes: "I've spent the vast bulk of my professional life standing guard on the citadel of free exercise and free speech, working to expand its walls and hardening its fortifications. But that citadel exists for a purpose beyond its mere continued existence. It is supposed to empower the church to fearlessly act as salt and light in a broken world."

BIBLICAL RESPONSES TO RELIGIOUS LIBERTY ISSUES

In Chapter 7 of my book, *The State of Our Nation: 7 Critical Issues*, I discuss religious liberty in the context of recent bias against Christians and the challenge of same-sex marriage. There I note that Christians must resist the temptation to withdraw from culture, choosing instead to take Christ to all nations as fervently and effectively as possible (Matthew 28:19).

Old Testament prophets clearly and consistently spoke out against the cultural sins of their day.

- Hosea condemned the "swearing, lying, murder, stealing, and committing adultery" of his culture

(Hosea 4:2). He also warned his society against drunkenness and sexual immorality (4:18) as well.

- Amos condemned enslavement (Amos 1:6–8), mistreatment of pregnant women (1:13) and the poor (2:6), sexual abuse (2:7), drunkenness (4:1), greed (5:11), and corruption (5:12).
- Obadiah warned against violence (v. 10).
- Micah condemned theft (Micah 2:1–2).

Much like the prophets of old, Paul was grieved by idolatry (Acts 17:16) and the sins of his day, many of which he listed specifically (Romans 1:18–32; Galatians 5:19–21). He had "great sorrow and unceasing anguish in [his] heart" (Romans 9:2) for his fellow Jews who had not made Jesus their Messiah. And he gave his life as a missionary to the Gentile world (Galatians 2:7–8).

In his cultural engagement, the apostle followed the example and ministry of our Lord. Jesus fed the hungry (John 6:1–14), healed the sick (Mark 1:33–34), and befriended the outcast (Luke 19:1–10). He taught us to do the same, calling us to be "salt" and "light" (Matthew 5:13–16). Both transform all they contact. As a result, the first Christians gave their goods to anyone who "had need" (Acts 2:45) and ministered to "the sick and those afflicted with unclean spirits" (Acts 5:16).

Clearly, they did more than "preach the gospel." Or, better said, they preached the gospel of God's love in actions as well as in words. They met felt need in order to meet spiritual need, earning the right to share the message of salvation in Christ.

What do we do when this spiritual calling conflicts with the secular authorities?

SERVING CHRIST AND CAESAR

It was Tuesday of Holy Week. Jesus was teaching the crowds gathered in the Temple corridors. Here, the unlikeliest of political coalitions came against him. The Pharisees hated the Roman occupation, but they also hated Jesus. They considered his grace-centered message to violate the Law and its demands. In their minds, he was a heretic whose influence must be stopped.

The Herodians supported the Roman occupation in every way. They and the Pharisees were in constant political conflict. But they also saw Jesus as a threat to the Empire's power. Like the Pharisees, they wanted him arrested or even killed. So, they "went out and plotted how to entangle him in his words" (Matthew 22:15). Luke gives us their underlying motive: "They hoped to catch Jesus in something he said, so that they might hand him over to the power and authority of the governor" (Luke 20:20 NIV).

The Pharisees sent some of their "disciples" to him (Matthew 22:16), students at one of the two Pharisaic theological seminaries in Jerusalem. Their youth might endear them to Jesus; at any event, they would be less recognizable to him than their leaders. After patronizing him with compliments, they asked their entrapping question: "Is it lawful to pay taxes to Caesar, or not?" (v. 17). Their grammar required a yes or no answer. And either would serve their purpose.

They pushed a very hot button. The "taxes" to which they referred were the poll-tax or "census" tax paid by all males over the age of fourteen and all females over the age of twelve. It was paid directly to the Emperor himself. And it required the use of a coin despised by the Jewish populace. This was the "denarius," a silver coin minted by the Emperor himself. It was the only Roman coin that claimed divine status for the Caesar. On one side, it pictured the head of Emperor Tiberius with the Latin inscription, "Tiberius Caesar son of the divine Augustus." On the other side, it pictured Pax, the Roman goddess of peace, with the Latin inscription "high priest." It was idolatrous in the extreme.

The tax it paid led to a Jewish revolt in AD 6, which established the Zealot movement. That movement eventually resulted in the destruction of Jerusalem and the Jewish nation in AD 70. At this time, that movement was growing in power and influence.

Thus, these schemers were asking Jesus to take a position on the most inflammatory issue of the day. If he said that it is right to pay taxes to Caesar, the public would turn from him in revolt and his influence would be at an end. If he said that it is *not* right to pay taxes to Caesar, Jesus would be a traitor to Rome, and the authorities would arrest and execute him. Either way, the hands of his opponents would be clean, and they would be rid of their enemy.

Here is Jesus' timeless answer: He asked for a denarius, and then he asked them, "Whose likeness and inscription is this?" (v. 20). They told him that it bore the image and inscription of Caesar. And he replied, "Render to Caesar the things that are Caesar's, and to God the things that are God's" (v. 21).

If taxes belong to the nation, pay them. If worship belongs to God, give it. Give to each what is due. Live in two countries, a citizen of both.

AMBASSADORS FOR CHRIST

Paul clarifies this image of citizenship when he called us "ambassadors for Christ" (2 Corinthians 5:20). An American ambassador lives in a foreign country under appointment by his president at home. They obey the laws of that nation. They give allegiance to its leaders and people. But they always have a second allegiance, an even higher allegiance to their home country and their leader. And if they must choose between the two, their loyalties are clear.

Like secular ambassadors, we are each to obey and support our governing authorities:

- "Let every person be subject to the governing authorities. For there is no authority except from God, and those that exist have been instituted by God" (Romans 13:1).

- "This is also why you pay taxes, for the authorities are God's servants, who give their full time to governing. Give everyone what you owe them: If you owe taxes, pay taxes; if revenue, then revenue; if respect, then respect; if honor, then honor" (Romans 13:6–7 NIV).

- "I urge that supplications, prayers, intercessions, and thanksgivings be made for all people, for kings and all who are in high positions, that we may lead a peaceful and quiet life, godly and dignified in every way" (1 Timothy 2:1–2; cf. Titus 3:1–2).

But we are also to obey and serve our Lord:

- "The fear of the Lord is the beginning of knowledge; fools despise wisdom and instruction" (Proverbs 1:7).

- "O kings, be wise; be warned, O rulers of the earth. Serve the Lord with fear, and rejoice with trembling. Kiss the Son, lest he be angry, and you perish in the way, for his wrath is quickly kindled. Blessed are all who take refuge in him" (Psalm 2:10–12).

This balance between reverence for Christ and respect for Caesar is captured in Peter's admonition: "Be subject for the Lord's sake to every human institution, whether it be to the emperor as supreme, or to governors as sent by him to punish those who do evil and to praise those who do good. . . . Honor everyone. Love the brotherhood. Fear God. Honor the emperor" (1 Peter 2:13–14, 17).

Note that we are to "honor" the emperor, but we are to "fear" only God. This means that if we must choose, we must choose our highest authority. We should come to this position only if we must, first seeking every means to obey the secular authorities while remaining true to our Lord. But there are times when we must declare with the apostles, "We must obey God rather than men" (Acts 5:29).

We are to love people, fear God, and honor the state. We are not to fear people or the state but God alone. In other words, serve your highest authority. When you can serve Christ and state, serve both. If you must choose, choose Christ.

In 2017, Chinese officials began ordering Christians to replace images of Jesus in their homes with posters of President Xi Jinping. I know believers in Cuba who have been told that they would have better jobs for themselves and schools for their children if they would renounce their commitment to Christ.

Even when we must oppose political leaders, we must do so in the character of Christ. It is imperative that we seek the empowering of the Spirit (Ephesians 5:18) in order to manifest the "fruit of the Spirit" (Galatians 5:22–23). We are to be respectful (Titus 3:2), considerate (1 Timothy 2:2), and reverent (1 Peter 3:15). We need to go to those with whom we disagree, speaking *to* them rather than *about* them (cf. Matthew 18:15). And we must never say *about* them what we would not say *to* them. We must refuse slander (cf. Psalm 101:5) and deceit (Exodus 20:16), "speaking the truth in love" always (Ephesians 4:15). It is urgent to remember that we represent the Lord in all we say and do.

But we are also to be bold (Acts 4:29; Ephesians 6:19), strong (1 Corinthians 16:13), and courageous (Philippians 1:28) in serving our Lord. When the Sanhedrin demanded that the apostles stop preaching the gospel, "Peter and the other apostles answered, 'We must obey God rather than men'" (Acts 5:29).

Serve your highest authority, always.

CONCLUSION

As David French noted, religious liberty is "supposed to empower the church to fearlessly act as salt and light in a broken world." He is right: religious freedom is a means to the end of spiritual freedom. American Christians can have complete liberty to preach the gospel and seek to win others to Christ, but if we do not preach the gospel and seek to win others to Christ, such liberty loses its eternal significance.

I am grateful for the advances with regard to religious liberty that David French discusses. However, I am concerned about the temptation to trust secular authorities to protect us from secular abuses. Court compositions can change quickly, and justices do not always rule in ways that are consistent with their previous decisions or perceived beliefs. In other words, the church must seize the opportunity that is ours today, using our religious freedom to share spiritual freedom in Christ as fully and effectively as possible.

And while politics is hardly the only—or even primary—way in which we should strive to do so, we are blessed to live in a country where it is an option. And our country is in desperate need of that spiritual freedom today.

In his Farewell Address, George Washington stated "The propitious smiles of heaven can never be expected on a nation that disregards the eternal rules of order and right which heaven itself has ordained." What if the spiritual future of our country depended upon the degree to which God's people incarnate and advance "the eternal rules of order and right" in our day?

It does.

A DISCUSSION GUIDE ON POLITICS AND RELIGIOUS LIBERTY

The following discussion guide may be used in a small group setting or for your personal time of devotion. We hope it helps you both better understand the topic and how God might want to use you, in your specific context, to be "salt and light" on this issue.

1. Do you consider yourself a political person? Why or why not?
2. Do you think the Bible addresses politics? If so, how?
3. How did God use political leaders in the Bible?
4. Outside of the examples listed in the article, what other political leaders did God use in the Bible?
5. How does God use political leaders today?
6. Why does the church seem to flourish when it's persecuted?
7. How have you prepared yourself, either now or in the past, for upcoming presidential voting days?
8. How can a Christian discern if God is calling them to serve in public office? (Alternately, why should more Christians consider lives of public service?)
9. Of the four ways listed to engage in politics, which do you routinely do? Why? Which do you fail to do? Why? What other ways might a Christian engage in the political process?
10. Is it ever OK for a Christian to disobey the government? If so, what should be taken into account?

11. Read Acts 5:17–33. Then consider the questions posed in this chapter's introduction:

    - Are America's Christians facing threats to our religious liberty on such a level that we must stand up at any cost? Have we reached that point where we must say to secular authorities, "We must obey God rather than men" (Acts 5:29)?
    - If you agree, name a few examples of recent threats to our religious liberty.
    - If you disagree, discuss why American Christians have not reached that point. Consider comparing our current cultural and governmental climate to that of the early Christians.

12. Do you believe that Christianity's influence on America is increasing or decreasing?

    - How would you argue your position?

13. In your personal life, do you tend to withdraw, withstand, or go forth into the culture? In other words, when pressed to take a stand on a sensitive cultural issue (e.g., abortion, same-sex marriage), do you retreat or stay silent? Do you answer only when asked? Are you proactive? Or even aggressive?

    - What are some of the benefits associated with each approach? What are some of the dangers?
    - How do you navigate the fine line of "speaking the truth in love" (Ephesians 4:15)?

What are some ways you can do that through both words and actions?

14. How can you be an "ambassador for Christ" in the following areas (2 Corinthians 5:20)?

- In your home?
- At your job?
- In your neighborhood?
- With your friends and family?
- At your church?
- Online?
- In the world at large?

15. How will God's word shape your politics going forward?

ABOUT DR. JIM DENISON

JIM DENISON, PHD, is a cultural theologian and the founder and CEO of Denison Ministries. He speaks biblically into significant cultural issues through The Daily Article at DenisonForum.org. He is the author of over 30 books, including *The Coming Tsunami: Why Christians Are Labeled Intolerant, Irrelevant, Oppressive, and Dangerous—and How We Can Turn the Tide*; *Respectfully, I Disagree: How to Be a Civil Person in an Uncivil Time*; and the *Biblical Insight to Tough Questions* series.

He has taught the philosophy of religion and apologetics at several seminaries. Dr. Denison serves as Resident Scholar for Ethics with Baylor Scott & White Health, where he addresses issues such as genetic medicine and reproductive science. He is a Senior Fellow with CEO Forum, 21st Century Wilberforce Initiative, the International Alliance of Christian Education, and Dallas Baptist University's Institute for Global Engagement.

He holds a Doctor of Philosophy and a Master of Divinity degree from Southwestern Baptist Theological Seminary. He also received an honorary Doctor of Divinity from Dallas Baptist University. Dr. Denison is the Theologian in Residence for the Baptist General Convention of Texas.

Prior to launching Denison Forum in 2009, he pastored churches in Texas and Georgia. Jim and his wife, Janet, have two married sons and four grandchildren.

ABOUT DENISON MINISTRIES

Denison Ministries is a Christian nonprofit that seeks to transform the culture through Christ-centered content. The ministry accomplishes that through four distinct brands:

- **Denison Forum** (denisonforum.org) offers a biblical and redemptive perspective on current events through *The Daily Article* email newsletter and podcast, *The Denison Forum Podcast*, and many books and online resources.

- **Christian Parenting** (christianparenting.org) provides practical and spiritual resources, including an expansive podcast network, to help parents raise children to know and love the Lord.

- **First15** (first15.org) leads Christians into a transformative personal encounter with God through devotional readings, worship videos, and guided prayers.

- **Foundations with Janet** (foundationswithjanet.org) offers Bible study resources with blogs, videos, and biblical content for individual and small-group use.

Learn more at DenisonMinistries.org.

NOTES

1. JESUS IS COMING SOON, RIGHT? WHAT DOES THE BIBLE SAY ABOUT THE END TIMES?

17 **"if you read history"**: C. S. Lewis, *Mere Christianity* (New York City: HarperCollins Publishers, 1952).

17 **"some people are so heavenly minded"**: This quote is traditionally attributed to Oliver Wendell Holmes, though there's debate about it.

17 **up until the early 1900s the two views were not recognized as being distinct**: Kim Riddlebarger, *A Case for Amillennialism: Understanding the End Times* (Grand Rapids: Baker Books, 2013).

2. THE CONTROVERSY OF BEING LEFT BEHIND: WHAT DOES THE BIBLE SAY ABOUT THE RAPTURE?

33 **The Greek word Paul used for "cry of command"**: D. Michael Martin, *1, 2 Thessalonians*, vol. 33, *The New American Commentary* (Nashville: Broadman & Holman Publishers, 1995), 151.

33 **"Their moment of judgment comes as a shock"**: Martin, 160.

34 **The Greek word *apantesin* . . . . Heralds of his coming would leave the city walls**: Martin, 153–155.

37 **The Greek phrase "to keep from"—*tereso ek***: Robert H. Guny, *Church and the Tribulation : A Biblical Examination of Posttribulationism* (Grand Rapids, Mich.: Zondervan, 2010), 54–61.

37 **"To say that a promise of deliverance"**: G. K. Beale, *The Book of Revelation: A Commentary on the Greek Text, New International Greek Testament Commentary* (Grand Rapids, MI; Carlisle, Cumbria: W.B. Eerdmans; Paternoster Press, 1999), 292.

3: DEFENDING YOURSELF WITHOUT ATTACKING YOUR WITNESS: WHAT DOES THE BIBLE SAY ABOUT SELF-DEFENSE AND GUN CONTROL?

45   **1.5 shootings every day:** "Gun Violence Archive." Gunviolencearchive.org. Gun Violence Archive, April 21, 2023. https://www.gunviolencearchive.org/.

45   **guns killed more young people than car accidents:** Dan Keating, "Guns Killed More Young People than Cars Did for the First Time in 2020," *Washington Post*, May 25, 2022, https://www.washingtonpost.com/health/2022/05/25/guns-kill-more-kids-than-cars/.

45   **the most common justification is self-defense:** Kim Parker, "The Demographics of Gun Ownership in the U.S.," Pew Research Center's Social & Demographic Trends Project (Pew Research Center, June 22, 2017), https://www.pewresearch.org/social-trends/2017/06/22/the-demographics-of-gun-ownership/.

46   **"'spiritual' sword of some kind":** Robert H. Stein, *Luke* (Nashville, Tenn.: B & H Publishing Group, 1992).

46   **"Jesus' statement . . . must be a way of emphasizing":** H. Franklin Paschall and Herschel H. Hobbs, *Teachers Bible Commentary* (Nashville: B & H Publishing Group, 2014).

47   **the disciples will want to get swords for protection:** John Walvoord, *Bible Knowledge Commentary: Old Testament and New Testament.* (Victor, 2002).

48   **"an absolutely universal principle":** Containing a General Introduction and the Gospel According to Matthew (A Commentary on the Holy Scriptures: Critical, Doctrinal and Homiletical, With Special Reference to Ministers and Students. Translated from the Greek, and Edited, With Additions Original and Selected., Volume I of the New Testament), https://www.amazon.com/Containing-Introduction-According-Commentary-Scriptures/dp/B000VLA1NE/

48	"observation that violence breeds violence": Craig L. Blomberg, *The New American Commentary Volume 22 - Matthew*. (Editorial: Nashville: B & H Publishing Group, 1992).
48	more admirable than responding with violence: Barclay Moon Newman and Philip C. Stine, *A Handbook on the Gospel of Matthew* (American Bible Society, 1992).
49	That phrase includes not only those who "keep the peace": Marvin R Vincent, *Word Studies in the New Testament*. (New York: Scribner, 1924).
50	"A righteous man would be characterized by": John Walvoord, *Bible Knowledge Commentary: Old Testament and New Testament*. (Victor, 2002).
51	"Striking a person on the right cheek": Craig L. Blomberg, *The New American Commentary Volume 22 - Matthew*. (Editorial: Nashville: B & H Publishing Group, 1992).
52	more easily caught during the day: John Walvoord, *Bible Knowledge Commentary: Old Testament and New Testament*. (Victor, 2002).
52	less likely to kill someone: Robert Jamieson, A R Fausset, and David Brown, *A Commentary Critical and Explanatory on the Whole Bible* (Grand Rapids, Mich.: Zondervan, 194, 1997).
52	more likely that someone entering your house is intruding: Douglas K Stuart, *The New American Commentary: Exodus* (Nashville, Tenn.: Broadman & Holman Publishers, 2006).
53	"did not allow unlimited freedom to the victim": Stuart.
54	"The natural impulse is to return injury for injury": Robert H Mounce, *Romans* (Nashville, Tenn.: Broadman & Holman, 2001).

57	**The number one reason cited for legally owning a gun:** Katherine Schaeffer, "Key Facts about Americans and Guns," Pew Research Center, September 13, 2023, https://www.pewresearch.org/short-reads/2023/09/13/key-facts-about-americans-and-guns/.
58	**such rifles have accounted for roughly 3 percent of firearm murders:** John Gramlich, "What the Data Says about Gun Deaths in the U.S.," Pew Research Center (Pew Research Center, April 26, 2023), https://www.pewresearch.org/short-reads/2023/04/26/what-the-data-says-about-gun-deaths-in-the-u-s/.
58	**its definition [of mass shootings] varies widely:** Rosanna Smart and Terry L. Schell, "Mass Shootings: Definitions and Trends," Rand.org, 2018, https://www.rand.org/research/gun-policy/analysis/essays/mass-shootings.html.
59	**According to the CDC in 2021:** John Gramlich, "What the Data Says about Gun Deaths in the U.S.," Pew Research Center (Pew Research Center, April 26, 2023), https://www.pewresearch.org/short-reads/2023/04/26/what-the-data-says-about-gun-deaths-in-the-u-s/.

4: "THE GLEAMING FUTURISTIC LAND OF OZ": WHAT DOES THE BIBLE SAY ABOUT ARTIFICIAL INTELLIGENCE?

65	**"This is going to change everything.... This is a Promethean moment":** Thomas L. Friedman, "Opinion | Our New Promethean Moment," *The New York Times*, March 21, 2023, sec. Opinion, https://www.nytimes.com/2023/03/21/opinion/artificial-intelligence-chatgpt.html.
66	**The term artificial intelligence was coined in the late 1950s:** Kevin Roose and Cade Metz, "How to Become an Expert on A.I.," *The New York Times*, March 27, 2023, sec. Technology, https://www.nytimes.com/article/ai-artificial-intelligence-chatbot.html.
67	**"chatbots" are "now poised to change our everyday lives":** Roose and Metz.

68   **GPT stands for generative pre-trained transformer:** Mark, "What Does GPT Stand for in ChatGPT?," MLYearning, March 27, 2023, https://www.mlyearning.org/what-does-gpt-stand-for-in-chat-gpt.

68   **"what ChatGPT is always fundamentally trying to do":** Stephen Wolfram, "What Is ChatGPT Doing ... and Why Does It Work?," writings.stephenwolfram.com, February 14, 2023, https://writings.stephenwolfram.com/2023/02/what-is-chatgpt-doing-and-why-does-it-work/?ref=thebrowser.com.

69   **Bill Gates predicts that AI will enable:** Bill Gates, "The Age of AI Has Begun," gatesnotes.com, March 21, 2023, https://www.gatesnotes.com/The-Age-of-AI-Has-Begun.

70   **test different arrangements of T-cells:** Ryan Denison PhD, "Will AI Cure Cancer?," Denison Forum, January 26, 2023, https://www.denisonforum.org/current-events/will-ai-cure-cancer/.

70   **"to sense the outside environment":** University of California-San Francisco, "How Artificial Intelligence Found the Words to Kill Cancer Cells," SciTechDaily, January 18, 2023, https://scitechdaily.com/how-artificial-intelligence-found-the-words-to-kill-cancer-cells/.

70   **"Cleerly," an AI-based evaluation system that scans the heart:** Rebekah Brandes, "New AI Could Help Predict and Prevent Heart Attacks," Nice News, March 11, 2023, https://nicenews.com/health-and-wellness/ai-predict-prevent-heart-attacks/.

70   **"What I am personally most excited about is":** Intelligencer Staff, "Sam Altman on What Makes Him 'Super Nervous' about AI," Intelligencer, March 23, 2023, https://nymag.com/intelligencer/2023/03/on-with-kara-swisher-sam-altman-on-the-ai-revolution.html.

71   **"AI is not as powerful as it might seem":** Kevin Roose and Cade Metz, "How to Become an Expert on A.I.," *The New York Times*, March 27, 2023, sec. Technology, https://www.nytimes.com/article/ai-artificial-intelligence-chatbot.html.

72   "the possibility that AIs will run out of control": Bill Gates, "The Age of AI Has Begun," gatesnotes.com, March 21, 2023, https://www.gatesnotes.com/The-Age-of-AI-Has-Begun.

72   "AI could develop a will of its own": Steve Yount, "Will Artificial Intelligence Achieve 'Godlike' Power? Wallace B. Henry Asks, 'Who Will Rule the Coming "Gods"?,'" Denison Forum, December 13, 2021, https://www.denisonforum.org/current-events/science-technology/will-artificial-intelligence-achieve-godlike-power-wallace-b-henry-asks-who-will-rule-the-coming-gods/.

74   "There will be AI": James Scimecca, "Right Back Where We Started From," The Dispatch, November 29, 2023, https://thedispatch.com/newsletter/morning/right-back-where-we-started-from/.

75   "I suddenly became aware of how vulnerable humanity will be": Wallace Henley and Otis Graf, *Who Will Rule the Coming "Gods"?: The Looming Spiritual Crisis of Artificial Intelligence* (Washington, D.C.: Vide Press, 2021).

76   "The truth is that our Western commitment to hedonism has proved empty and damaging": Os Guinness, *Signals of Transcendence* (InterVarsity Press, 2023).

5: THE PARDONABLE SIN: WHAT DOES THE BIBLE SAY ABOUT SUICIDE?

79   over 700,000 people take their own life every year: World Health Organization, "World Suicide Prevention Day 2023," www.who.int, 2023, https://www.who.int/campaigns/world-suicide-prevention-day/2023.

79   a suicide occurs every forty seconds: "Stay Here," Stay Here, n.d., https://www.stayhere.live/.

79   Miss USA Cheslie Kryst died by suicide: Jim Denison PhD, "Former Miss USA Cheslie Kryst Posted Cryptic Message before Her Death by Suicide," Denison Forum, February 1, 2022, https://www.denisonforum.org/daily-

article/former-miss-usa-cheslie-kryst-posted-cryptic-message-before-her-death-by-suicide/.

80 **According to Seacoast Church:** Bob Smietana, "Friends mourn Darrin Patrick, megachurch pastor and author, who died of apparent 'self-inflicted gunshot wound'," Religion News Service, last modified May 8, 2020, https://religionnews.com/2020/05/08/friends-mourn-darrin-patrick-megachurch-pastor-and-author-who-died-unexpectedly/.

80 **suicide rates rose until 2018:** Centers for Disease Control and Prevention, "Suicide Data and Statistics," www.cdc.gov (CDC, August 10, 2023), https://www.cdc.gov/suicide/suicide-data-statistics.html.

80 **they have risen due to the pandemic:** Erika Edwards, "Suicides Are Rising Again, Especially among Young Men," NBC News, September 30, 2022, https://www.nbcnews.com/health/health-news/2-year-decline-suicide-rates-rise-rcna49766.

80 **suicide is the second-leading cause of death for Americans ages ten to thirty-four:** "Suicide by Age | Suicide Prevention Resource Center," Sprc.org, 2017, http://www.sprc.org/scope/age.

80 **In the UK, it is the leading cause of death among:** "Leading Causes of Death, UK - Office for National Statistics," www.ons.gov.uk, n.d., https://www.ons.gov.uk/peoplepopulationandcommunity/healthandsocialcare/causesofdeath/articles/leadingcausesofdeathuk/2001to2018#uk-leading-causes-of-death-by-age-group.

80 **Suicide rates have grown exponentially for women since 1999:** "NPR Choice Page," Npr.org, 2019, https://www.npr.org/sections/health-shots/2016/04/22/474888854/suicide-rates-climb-in-u-s-especially-among-adolescent-girls.

81 **more than half of the people who died by suicide did not have a known mental health condition:** CDC, "Suicide Rising across the US," Centers for Disease Control and Prevention, November 27, 2018, https://www.cdc.gov/vitalsigns/suicide.

81 **direct link between anxiety and opioid use:** Nick Zagorski, "Many Prescription Opioids Go to Adults With Depression, Anxiety," Psychiatric News, last modified August 17, 2017, https://psychnews.psychiatryonline.org/doi/full/10.1176/appi.pn.2017.8a13.

81 **two to three times more likely:** "Substance Use," Anxiety & Depression Association of America, https://adaa.org/understanding-anxiety/co-occurring-disorders/substance-abuse.

81 **Anxiety is linked to:** "Pain, anxiety, and depression," Harvard Health Publishing: Harvard Medical School," last modified June 5, 2019, https://www.health.harvard.edu/mind-and-mood/pain-anxiety-and-depression.

81 **related anxiety directly to suicide:** Claire Mokrysz, "Patients with anxiety disorders are more likely to have suicidal thoughts and actions, says recent review," National Elf Service, The Mental Elf, last modified September 10, 2013, https://www.nationalelfservice.net/mental-health/anxiety/patients-with-anxiety-disorders-are-more-likely-to-have-suicidal-thoughts-and-actions-says-recent-review/.

81 **over a third of Americans "show symptoms of anxiety, depression, or both":** Alyssa Fowers and William Wan, "A Third of Americans Now Show Signs of Clinical Anxiety or Depression, Census Bureau Finds amid Coronavirus Pandemic," *Washington Post*, May 26, 2020, sec. Health, https://www.washingtonpost.com/health/2020/05/26/americans-with-depression-anxiety-pandemic/.

81 **Twenty percent of high school students report serious thoughts of suicide:** National Alliance on Mental Illness, "What You Need to Know about Youth Suicide | NAMI: National Alliance on Mental Illness," www.nami.org, n.d., https://www.nami.org/Your-Journey/Kids-Teens-and-Young-Adults/What-You-Need-to-Know-About-Youth-Suicide.

82 **eight times as likely:** Jean Twenge, "Coronavirus pandemic takes staggering toll on mental health in US," Live Science, last modified May 8, 2020, https://www.livescience.com/coronavirus-pandemic-mental-health-toll.html.

83	**What does the Bible say about suicide?:** Sources for this study include: *Catechism of the Catholic Church*, second edition English translation; the National Center for Injury Prevention and Control (www.ced.gov/ncipc); . T. Clemons, "Suicide," *International Standard Bible Encyclopedia*, ed. Geoffrey W. Bromiley(Grand Rapids: Eerdmans, 1988) 4:652–3; A. J. Droge, "Suicide," *The Anchor Bible Dictionary*, ed. David Noel Freedman (New York: Doubleday, 1992) 6:225–31; Milton A. Gonsalves, *Fagothey's Right and Reason: Ethics in Theory and Practice*, 9th ed. (Columbus: Merrill Publishing Company, 1989) 246–8; the Suicide Awareness Voices of Education (www.save.org); and the American Association of Suicidology (www.suicidology.org).
90	**Catechism of the Catholic Church:** *Catechism of the Catholic Church: Second Edition*, https://www.usccb.org/sites/default/files/flipbooks/catechism/.
93	**legal in ten US states:** CNN Editorial Research, "Physician-Assisted Suicide Fast Facts," CNN, last modified June 11, 2020, https://www.cnn.com/2014/11/26/us/physician-assisted-suicide-fast-facts/index.html.
93	**PAD is available to one in five Americans:** Alexander Gelfand, "TAKING A STAND ON PHYSICIAN-ASSISTED SUICIDE: Seeking a More Engaged Role to Aid Terminally Ill Patients," Think, Case Western Reserve University, https://case.edu/think/spring2017/physician-assisted-suicide.html#.YHSf4ehKjiP.
93	**"doctors should be allowed by law":** Megan Brenan, "Americans' Strong Support for Euthanasia Persists," Gallup, last modified May 31, 2018, https://news.gallup.com/poll/235145/americans-strong-support-euthanasia-persists.aspx.
94	**"Euthanasia" is derived from the Greek words:** For further discussion of the terms and issues involved in euthanasia, see David K. Clark and Robert V. Rakestraw, *Readings in Christian Ethics* (Grand Rapids: Baker, 1996) 2:95–101. Other sources which have informed my study include David Theo Goldberg, *Ethical Theory and Social Issues: Historical Texts and Contemporary*

Readings (New York: Holt, Rinehart and Winston, Inc., 1988) 388–419; and Robert D. Orr, Dvaid L. Schiedermayer, and David B. Biebel, *Life and Death Decisions* (Colorado Springs, Colorado: NavPress, 1990) 151–65.

96   **10,000 to 25,000 PVS patients:** Kenneth V. Iserson, "Persistent Vegetative State," Encyclopedia of Death and Dying, http://www.deathreference.com/Nu-Pu/Persistent-Vegetative-State.html.

98   **the scriptural description of humanity:** A helpful introduction to this complex subject is Robert V. Rakestraw, "The Persistent Vegetative State and the Withdrawal of Nutrition and Hydration," in Clark and Rakestraw, 2:116–31.

102 **twelve "suicide warning signs":** "Injury Prevention & Control," Centers for Disease Control and Prevention, last modified March 9, 2021, https://www.cdc.gov/injury/features/be-there-prevent-suicide/index.html.

103 **"The Kate Spade Conversation":** Janet Denison, "The Kate Spade Conversation," Christian Parenting, last modified June 7, 2018, http://www.christianparenting.org/articles/kate-spade-conversation/.

104 **the following indicators help buffer people:** "Suicide Prevention: Risk and Protective Factors," Centers for Disease Control and Prevention, last modified January 25, 2021, https://www.cdc.gov/suicide/factors/index.html?CDC_AA_refVal=https%3A%2F%2Fwww

104 **"Mental pain is less dramatic":** C. S. Lewis, *The Problem of Pain* (United States, HarperOne, 2001), 161.

105 **"There are no *ordinary* people":** C. S. Lewis, *The Weight of Glory* (United States: HarperOne), 2009.

6: THE MORAL ISSUE OF OUR TIME: WHAT DOES THE BIBLE SAY ABOUT ABORTION?

110 **nearly 70 percent of Americans support at least some access to abortion:** Gallup Inc, "Where Do Americans Stand on Abortion?," Gallup.com (Gallup, September 29, 2020), https://news.gallup.com/poll/321143/americans-stand-abortion.aspx.

112 **several specific reasons why she might choose abortion:** "Roe v. Wade / Excerpts from Majority Opinion," Landmark Cases, last modified August 20, 2020, https://www.landmarkcases.org/assets/site_18/files/roe_v_wade/teacher/pdf/decision_majority_excerpts_roe_teacher.pdf.

120 **"The embryo has its own autonomy":** Karl Barth, *Church Dogmatics* (Edinburgh: T & T Clark, 1985 [1961]) 3.4.416.

124 **"The law seems rather to mean":** Flavius Josephus, *The Works of Josephus* (United States: Lindsay & Blakiston, 1859), 314.

133 **abortion must be legal as a remedy:** Virginia Ramey Mollenkott, "Reproductive Choice: Basic to Justice for Women" in *Readings in Christian Ethics: Volume 2: Issues and Applications*, eds. David K. Clark and Robert V. Rakestraw (Baker Academic: 2008).

137 **"Your opinion [in Roe v. Wade] stated":** Mother Teresa in *Speeches that Changed the World* (United States: Westminster John Knox Press, 1999), 431.

138 **"It is a poverty to decide":** "7 of Our Favorite Mother Teresa Quotes," March for Life, last modified August 31, 2017, https://marchforlife.org/mother-teresa-favorite-quotes/.

138 **"the greatest destroyer of peace today":** Mother Teresa of Calcutta, "Whatsoever You Do...": Speech of Mother Teresa of Calcutta to the National Prayer Breakfast, Washington, DC, February 3, 1994, https://www.priestsforlife.org/library/4386-whatsoever-you-do.

7: THE GREATEST SIN IN AMERICA: WHAT DOES THE BIBLE SAY ABOUT RACISM?

145 **"a majority of Americans"**: Juliana Menasce Horowitz, Anna Brown, and Kiana Cox, "How Americans see the state of race relations," Pew Research Center, last modified April 9, 2019, https://www.pewresearch.org/social-trends/2019/04/09/how-americans-see-the-state-of-race-relations/

145 **60 percent of hate crimes:** "2016 Hate Crime Statistics Released," FBI, last modified November 13, 2017, https://www.fbi.gov/news/stories/2016-hate-crime-statistics.

145 **"prejudice, discrimination, or antagonism":** "racism," Lexico, https://www.lexico.com/definition/racism.

146 **"having little of Humanitie":** Sean P. Harvey, "Ideas of Race in Early America," Oxford Research Encyclopedias: American History, last modified April 5, 2016, https://oxfordre.com/americanhistory/view/10.1093/acrefore/9780199329175.001.0001/acrefore-9780199329175-e-262.

146 **"Negro's were Beasts":** Harvey.

149 **Studies show that racism persists in America:** Jeff Nesbit, "Institutional Racism Is Our Way of Life," *U.S. News & World Report*, last modified May 6, 2015, https://www.usnews.com/news/blogs/at-the-edge/2015/05/06/institutional-racism-is-our-way-of-life.

149 **"my church is involved with racial reconciliation":** Ruth Moon, "Does the Gospel Mandate Racial Reconciliation? White Pastors Agree More Than Black Pastors," *Christianity Today*, last modified December 16, 2014, https://www.christianitytoday.com/news/2014/december/does-gospel-mandate-racial-reconciliation-lifeway-kainos.html.

149 **"people of color are often put at a social disadvantage":** "people of color are often put at a social disadvantage," Barna, last modified May 5, 2016, https://www.barna.com/research/black-lives-matter-and-racial-tension-in-america/#.V45Hf5MrKb8.

149   **81 percent of America's Protestant churches:** Bob Smietana, "Sunday Morning Segregation: Most Worshipers Feel Their Church Has Enough Diversity," *Christianity Today,* last modified January 15, 2015, https://www.christianitytoday.com/news/2015/january/sunday-morning-segregation-most-worshipers-church-diversity.html.

150   **90 percent of Protestant pastors:** Smietana.

153   **"We know many among ourselves":** Pope Saint Clement I, trans. by Alexander Roberts and James Donaldson, "First Epistle to the Corinthians," Ch. 55, Logos Library, http://www.logoslibrary.org/clement1/corinthians/55.html.

153   **"Do not despise either male or female slaves":** "St. Ignatius of Antiocha To Polycarp, Chapter IV-Exhortations," The epistle to Polycarp, IntraText, http://www.intratext.com/IXT/ENG0861/_P5.HTM.

160   **As Dr. Evans shows:** Tony Evans, "Are Black People Cursed? The Curse of Ham," eternal perspective ministries, last modified January 18, 2010, https://www.epm.org/resources/2010/Jan/18/are-black-people-cursed-curse-ham/.

162   **"if anyone would like to acquire humility":** C. S. Lewis, *Mere Christianity* (1952; repr., Harpercollins Publishers, 2017).

163   **"In some ways, it's super simple":** William Wan and Sarah Kaplan, "Why are people still racist? What science says about America's race problem.," *Washington Post,* last modified August 14, 2017, https://www.washingtonpost.com/news/speaking-of-science/wp/2017/08/14/why-are-people-still-racist-what-science-says-about-americas-race-problem/.

164   **"Americans, I think, have a great advantage":** Julissa Higgins, "Read George W. Bush's Speech at the Dallas Shooting Memorial Service," *Time,* last modified July 12, 2016, https://time.com/4403510/george-w-bush-speech-dallas-shooting-memorial-service/.

165   **"One of the real tragedies today":** Tony Evans, "Opinion: America's current violence can be traced to Christians'

failures," *Washington Post*, last modified July 9, 2016, https://www.washingtonpost.com/news/acts-of-faith/wp/2016/07/09/americas-current-violence-can-be-traced-to-christians-failures/.

166 **"We who hated and destroyed"**: Justin Martyr, "The First Apology," New Advent, https://www.newadvent.org/fathers/0126.htm.

166 **"Through the perfection of his love"**: Mayor, Joseph Bickersteth., Hort, Fenton John Anthony. Clement of Alexandria, *Miscellanies Book VII: The Greek Text with Introduction, Translation, Notes, Dissertations and Indices* (United Kingdom: Macmillan, 1902), 135.

166 **"We love one another"**: Minucius Felix, "Ante-Nicene Fathers, Vol IV: The Octavius of Minucius Felix.," St-Takla.org: Coptic Orthodox Church Heritage, https://st-takla.org/books/en/ecf/004/0040034.html.

166 **"See how they love one another"**: Christianity.com Editorial Staff, "What Were Early Christians Like?," Christianity.com, last modified May 3, 2010, https://www.christianity.com/church/church-history/timeline/1-300/what-were-early-christians-like-11629560.html.

8: THE CALL TO TRANSFORMATIONAL GOOD: WHAT DOES THE BIBLE SAY ABOUT POLITICS AND RELIGIOUS LIBERTY?

171 **"My walk is a public one"**: "William Wilberforce: 171 politician," *Christianity Today*, https://www.christianitytoday.com/history/people/activists/william-wilberforce.html.

171 **"Let the consequences be"**: *Christianity Today*.

172 **"One of the turning events in the history of the world"**: *Christianity Today*.

172 **"the art or science of government"**: "politics," Merriam-Webster, last modified April 7, 2021, https://www.merriam-webster.com/dictionary/politics.

172 **four kinds of political systems:** "Political system,"

Wikipedia, last modified March 31, 2021, https://en.wikipedia.org/wiki/Political_system.

173 **"Politicians are the same all over"**: "Khrushchev Needles Peking," *Chicago Tribune*, August 22, 1963.

175 **nearly all US presidents . . . Christian faith:** Aleksandra Sandstrom, "Biden is only the second Catholic president, but nearly all have been Christians," Pew Research Center, last modified January 20, 2021, https://www.pewresearch.org/fact-tank/2021/01/20/biden-only-second-catholic-president-but-nearly-all-have-been-christians-2/.

177 **China is the world's largest producer of Bibles:** Eleanor Albert, "Christianity in China," Council on Foreign Religions, last modified October 11, 2018, https://www.cfr.org/backgrounder/christianity-china.

177 **more Christians than members of the Communist Party:** Tsukasa Hadano, "China's Christians keep the faith, rattling the country's leaders," Nikkei Asia, last modified September 10, 2019.

177 **"more Protestants in church in China than in all of Europe"**: Serene Fang, "A Brief History of the Christianity in China," Frontline/World, https://www.pbs.org/frontlineworld/stories/china_705/history/china.html.

189 **ordering Christians to replace images of Jesus:** Kate Shellnutt, "China Tells Christians to Replace Images of Jesus with Communist President," *Christianity Today*, last modified November 17, 2017, https://www.christianitytoday.com/news/2017/november/china-christians-jesus-communist-president-xi-jinping-yugan.html.

191 **"The propitious smiles of heaven"**: George Washington, "Washington's Inaugural Address of 1789," National Archives and Records Administration, https://www.archives.gov/exhibits/american_originals/inaugtxt.html.

182 **"Singing in church is a biblical mandate"**: Chace Beech, "Three California churches sue Newsom over singing ban," *Los Angeles Times*, last modified July 16, 2020, https://www.latimes.com/california/story/2020-07-16/california-churches-sue-newsom-singing-ban.

183 **"contains a provision specifically designed to protect the autonomy of religious organizations":** David French, "The True Extent of Religious Liberty in America, Explained," The Dispatch, last modified June 21, 2020, https://frenchpress.thedispatch.com/p/the-true-extent-of-religious-liberty.